BETWEEN THE LINES

Between the lines *provides a safe and practical introduction to the concepts of family constellation and carries the essence of "Hellinger Sciencia" into practical applications, meditations and exercises for easy esoteric explorations of you and your family. Nikki Mackay shows us the way to read between the lines of our inner and outer responses to family and relationships in general. Nikki prepares us for inner exploration by giving us living examples of the invisible esoteric influences affecting many famous lives. You are sure to enhance deeper levels of being able to understand the multidimensional human mystery you are, by walking a while with Nikki into your family field.*

Sadhana Kay Needham
www.familyconstellationeducation.com

Have you ever felt tormented by negative family patterns, or felt invisible or excluded? One possible contributor to such disharmony is long-standing unspoken disunity between family members – both living and dead. Nikki Mackay introduces us to family constellation therapy in her fascinating book, Between the Lines, *which helps us recognize, explore, and heal ancestral energy patterns at the root of our deepest issues and pain. Mackay invites us to see how we can connect to and bring healing to all generations of our ancestors by bearing compassionate witness to even the darkest family secrets.* Between the Lines *lovingly guides us to find the balance point in family dramas by showing how we can hold our own place in our family tree, with all around us at peace, with everyone having an assured place and a right to belong.*

Cynthia Sue Larson
Author of *Aura Advantage, and Reality Shifts: When Consciousness Changes the Physical World*

A fascinating concept well worth exploring in NIkki's brand new book.
Jacky Newcomb
Best Selling Author. One of the UK's leading Paranormal-Experience Experts, specialising in; Angels, The Afterlife, Between Lives, Psychic Children etc www.jackynewcomb.co.uk

Nikk's background in the field of science lends itself to this subject and she has managed to weave a tapestry of family ancestral patterns and constellations together beautifully in this book. It's such an easy read yet provides thought provoking information while dispelling the inner mystery of family life – so much so that makes you want to go and experience her workshops for yourself. This is a wonderful knowledge based piece of work and a gift to all of us.
Joan Charles
Author of *An Angel Walked Beside Me* - Scottish Sun Oracle Columnist

Between the Lines

Healing the Individual & Ancestral Soul with Family Constellation

Between the Lines

Healing the Individual & Ancestral Soul with Family Constellation

Nikki Mackay

BOOKS

Winchester, UK
Washington, USA

First published by O-Books, 2012
O-Books is an imprint of John Hunt Publishing Ltd., Laurel House, Station Approach,
Alresford, Hants, SO24 9JH, UK
office1@o-books.net
www.o-books.com

For distributor details and how to order please visit the 'Ordering' section on our website.

Text copyright: Nikki Mackay 2010

ISBN: 978 1 84694 447 5

A CIP catalogue record for this book is available from the British Library.

Design: Stuart Davies

Printed and bound by CPI Group (UK) Ltd., Croydon, CR0 4YY
Printed in the USA by Offset Paperback Mfrs, Inc

We operate a distinctive and ethical publishing philosophy in all
areas of our business, from our global network of authors to
production and worldwide distribution.

CONTENTS

Acknowledgements

I'd like to thank the clients who have allowed their stories to be told. Heartfelt thanks to my teachers who have supported me and pushed me on. To all the friends who read and reread providing feedback and encouragement a big 'thank you', the chocolate is on its way. Finally deep gratitude to my family, my husband and son for the encouragement and patience they have shown as this book emerged.

Preface

Each of us has a mother and a father. This is a basic fact that often seems to need no understanding, explanation, or consideration. We all too often take that fact for granted, yet our beginnings and family circumstances shape the very foundation of our life and future potentials for success or failure, health, illness, happiness or misery. The quality of the life we live is rooted in family facts. Knowingly or unknowingly we all hold a set of images from our family that colour our actions, decisions and responses for years and even generations to come. The problem is that those images we carry are often fictitious interpretations of the facts. These images become embedded in body, mind and spirit, and are made of memory. Memory that is often polluted by shock, trauma, blind love, loyalty and the interpretations of the child we were then. These memories are imprinted deeply into what Dr. Daniel Siegal refers to as our "neurobiology." Seigal has coined the phrase neuro science in his attempt to marry the physical responses, of the neurobiology of the body and brain, with mindfulness and growth of awareness. He recognises that neural integration is at the heart of every therapeutic process attempting to heal or transform human energy states. How then do we purify an old memory, change our interpretations, reframe our understandings or recreate new life affirming images that are able to take us forward into a creative future? We need to learn to read between the lines, between the images and between the habitual neuro responses our very own brain, body and nervous system.

The author of this book, Nikki Mackay, shows us the way to read between the lines of our inner and outer responses to family and relationships in general. Nikki prepares us for inner exploration by giving us living examples of the invisible esoteric influences affecting many famous lives. She also provides examples

I

from her very own sessions as a family constellation therapist using psychic insight to widen our understanding of invisible family dynamics. We learn that hidden family secrets can have devastating effects upon family systems. Through the information and soul searching processes outlined in this book we are able to gain a powerful and renewed sense of connection to our genetic-psychic linage. It imparts insights that have the potential to transform psychological and emotional suffering into a state of well-being and self-empowerment.

Perhaps you have just decided it is time for you to trace your family history and create a family tree; or you are seeking and searching answers to unanswered family and personal questions. Maybe you are simply curious about family constellation work or passionate about ancestral journeys, or a facilitator of the same. Whatever your reason for finding yourself on this page you are sure to enhance deeper levels of being able to understand the multidimensional human mystery you are, by walking a while with Nikki into your family field. Between the lines provides a safe and practical introduction to the basic concepts of family constellation work as developed by Bert Hellinger. "Between the Lines" carries the essence of "Hellinger Sciencia" into practical applications, meditations and exercises for easy esoteric explorations of you and your family. You will be introduced to the origins of family constellation, and encouraged to explore your very own inner world, of both physical and metaphysical sensations provoked by your journeying. You will learn how to self manage conflict within relationships affecting work, family and self, that separate instead of integrate. The inner journeys provided by this book provide an opportunity for immediate understanding; as awareness and neural integration opens the heart's innate ability to transform memory into conscious purposeful movement beyond mind itself. The reader is assisted to recognize, explore and heal personal and ancestral energy patterns via examples and exercises designed to strengthen intuition and clear the nervous system of trapped energy held by conditioning, blind love and loyalty. Static mental patterns of the mind begin to dissolve, as awareness and intuition surface out of the natural orders of soul revealed via the inner journeying here.

Between the Lines can complement an array of traditional allopathic and contemplative and alternative healing disciplines. Taking the reader by the hand, step by step, it provides multiple opportunities to discuss, identify and develop the strengths and weaknesses of family connections and separations. It shows us a new way to look, and attune our psyche to the inherent esoteric powers of intuition we already possess. The book puts into perspective and brings to the surface what we know intuitively but are unable to define. The use of neuro based mindfulness during much of the inner journeying is created to subtly release nervous rigidity and energy blocks that prevent connection to life force. If you are a family constellation facilitator I recommend this book as an introduction to intuitive family constellation work as a pre session or training tool. For others this book provides a simple and accurate map to guide the inner explorer into the rich landscape of inner ancestral geography. The whole purpose of this book is to guide you into a direct experience of your personal interiority. The maps can help you to find your way back to your soul. Once you are able to trust the experience of your family soul, the map is no longer needed.

Sadhana Kay Needham
www.familyconstellationeducation.com

Introduction

We spin an intricate web of connection and entanglement throughout our life from birth to death, interweaving through our bonds with our family, our friendships and our intimate relationships. Have you ever wondered why you do the things you do? Why you feel drawn to a particular path? Or perhaps why your intimate relationships and friendships turn out the way in which they do? Think about your life so far... What springs to mind? Your family and work? Your friends and relationships? Perhaps your successes and disappointments. Can you see a familiar pattern or rhythm appearing before you as you look?

I am constantly amazed at the things that are forgotten or suppressed within a family. Within every family there are secrets that are never spoken of. There are crimes and violence that have been perpetrated both within and outside of the family. All these things are swept under the carpet, but the unseen and unspoken have a habit of making themselves heard further down the line. So if you are interested in moving forward and truly seeing what is there within your family tree, come take a walk with me...

The memories of those that have gone before you are in your blood, the very souls are within your soul and family constellation and ancestral patterning is a way of accessing the fabric of this family soul as it weaves its way through and beyond you.

The complexities of human relationships are endlessly fascinating. The interaction between parent and child, brother and sister, husband and wife can become all encompassing and all consuming. The most natural and seemingly simplest way to analyse our relationships with our nearest and dearest is from our own perspective, thinking perhaps only of how we are connected as individuals and not taking into account outside influences.

We are not isolated, we are connected. The fabric of our soul is linked with that of our family. It is woven within the hearts of our mother, our father, our siblings and our ancestors. When we think only in terms of ourselves as individuals, we lose sight of who we really are and our sense of self and place. To truly be connected with who you are and to stand strong and independently we must first look to where we come from. Should we not get on with our family, if we have had a difficult childhood or suffered trauma within the family, a natural instinct can be to disconnect and disengage, denying our link to all that pains us and seeking freedom and identity via another path. In doing this we risk disengaging from life itself. As we deny our place within our family, we often sabotage our place within our emotional relationships and working lives. If we cut out part of our family, say the masculine line or the feminine line, we are cutting out and denying part of our self. The likelihood also is that the more we try to separate ourselves from a particular individual, fate or entanglement within the family the closer we wrap the vines of the entanglement around our very soul. The memories of our ancestors run through our blood.

In the same way that stars form patterns called constellations, family members and how they interact with each other create behavioural patterns that can be traced through the ancestral lines. Family constellation work, established by Bert Hellinger is based on the principle of the inter-connectedness of all things so that each person within a family, going back generation upon generation, has an equal place of belonging within that family. When someone in the family is excluded, or there is an event or entanglement that is not seen or acknowledged by the rest, then this has an effect on the family as a whole. Patterns, events and burdens from the past are carried down and are repeated through generations, leaving an emotional, physical and spiritual imprint on the individual as they follow the fates of those who have gone before. The events of previous generations that can impact in the present are many and far reaching. Situations of war, violent behaviour or experience of violence, murder, early deaths, loss of children, abortion, adoption, addictions, missing parents and siblings, and previous relationships all leave an imprint on the family if left unseen and unacknowledged.

Family constellations and ancestral patterns work provides an invaluable opportunity to explore these patterns and bring to light that which needs to be seen. I work with both individuals and groups listening to the ancestors and helping individuals bring peace and balance to their family field, and in turn, to allow them to truly take their own place within their family. Our perception of 'ancestors' is often that they are far-off figures, in the distance and unreachable. Into each intimate and personal relationship you embark on, you carry with you the energy and entanglements of your mother and father and the masculine and feminine lines of your ancestors.

As we connect with others, as we fall in love, we weave the web of the family lines and the ancestors with us. We take all that we are into our relationships as do those that we love. The patterns within our love lives can be confusingly complicated when viewed from an individual and personal perspective but when we can step back and view the ancestral web we can perhaps see a way forward.

We tend to find our own and other peoples' relationship dynamics particularly fascinating. If a friend asked you to describe your relationship history, or for details about your current relationship with your partner or spouse, what would you say? Maybe you would discuss the traits and foibles of your current partner or possibly express regret or relief at the demise of a previous relationship. Perhaps you would talk about any children you might have. Would you think about the parental and familial influences on your relationship? Would you think about your own previous relationships as having an impact? When we make an emotional bond to somebody through a committed relationship, an engagement or a marriage we create a bond that cannot be broken, this bond is even stronger when a couple has a child together. When a relationship ends, for whatever reason, any unfinished business or unacknowledged happenings from the relationship are carried forward to any subsequent relationships, and very often the events or happenings will repeat themselves.

Patterns and entanglements from previous relationships can take many forms, but some of the most common involve the experience of a string of short or long term monogamous relationships that end within a similar length of time. Some find themselves unable to commit within a relationship, perhaps when a certain point in the relationship is reached, the urge to end the connection becomes irresistible. Oftentimes the repetitive occurrence of betrayal, lack of commitment, or dominating partners will flag up entanglements within the family system. Other indicators include an inability to 'let go' of emotions connected to previous partners, this can be highlighted and further complicated by difficulty in communication within any subsequent relationships. Experiencing difficulty communicating and connecting with your children can be devastating and isolating for both the parent and the child. Sometimes it can feel as though the harder we try, the harder we push the more difficult the relationship becomes. How would you feel if I said that this experience often indicates a tie to a previous relationship where the children are unconsciously drawn to either the previous partner or the ancestors? In this instance your connection to your children (as well as your new partner) is 'blocked' by the link to the past where you and in some cases your off-spring are 'seeing' them rather than those around you. They can be representing that which you do not want to see or simply cannot see. This in turn flows forward and has an effect on their own relationship patterns and choices when they come of age. And so the web continues. In 'Between the Lines' we explore the hidden dynamics within familial relationships, intimate relationships as well as your patterns for success and creativity within your working life. Is your life destined by the stars? Perhaps we should look at the family tree instead... We will walk through ancestral and family patterns that have impacted and affected our relationships, both past and present, using examples from my clinical practice as well as exploring the dynamics of the famous and the infamous. By giving an appropriate place to our previous relationships, acknowledging and seeing them as they truly were, without guilt or blame, as well as by acknowledging who we are, who we were and where our root and place in our family lies, we can begin to free ourselves from the fates of the past. There will also be opportunities for you to uncover and work with your own family patterns.

My work with family and ancestral patterns is something that has evolved through the various different aspects of my working and personal life. It is something I am incredibly passionate about. For me it started with my intuitive work through the Tarot where I was able to 'see' the patterns at play within an individual's life and trace the pattern back to the very root through the family tree. This then took me to explore ways in which the root of the issue could perhaps be 'healed' or cleared and so I began to work intensively with energy healing alongside my intuitive work. At the time of my immersion into the world of energy healing, I was also working as a Medical Physicist. I created an opportunity to study the effects of energy healing on the nervous system as part of my Masters degree and published my findings within the medical and new age communities. I still felt there was more to explore in terms of the effects of previous generations on an individual's life. At this point I discovered the work of Bert Hellinger and his Family Constellation work. I haven't looked back since. On discovering Hellinger's work it all clicked into place and I have been combining my intuitive and energetic skills with the constellation work to great effect. For me it is like taking an intuitive walk through the family tree. Stopping and looking for those missing souls who are not seen, who have no voice and bearing witness to their life stories in order that they be acknowledged and seen by the rest of the family, in order that they are given their place. If they can be seen, be heard and be acknowledged then all of those entangled within the family become free. When the dead are not at peace, are not respected and given their place then they have an influence over the living as if they were still alive themselves.

The work is about bearing witness to the past and all that has been. With family constellation work you weave with the very fabric of the soul. The soul from a child just created and not destined for the world and the soul of a ninety year old who has seen and fought, lived and loved, both belong equally to the family field and each have a place. The souls that have been excluded and the souls that have been cherished both have an equal place. Life is precious and of value. All have a right to be seen, to take their place, their story told. Bear witness with me.

Chapter One

Walking through the Family tree

The purpose of working with your ancestors and family lineage is to allow you to reconnect with who you are, to take your place and to 'remember' who you are within your soul. Seeing and acknowledging those who have gone before you can pave the way for those that will follow in your footsteps.

When working with individuals I find that I see family lines unfolding behind them like swirls of smoke. I often see the break or the 'knot' in the line that is taking the energy. Very often this is something that has happened generations before and has been perpetuated and strengthened by more recent events within the family or in that particular aspect of the family line. It is important for the event or action to be acknowledged as the root cause. Very often it is more comfortable to view our patterns of behaviour and choices from a distance, and it is easier to avoid dealing with what we need to clear if it is something that is seen to be connected to the past. My prior work as a historical medium is something that I find incredibly useful within the constellation setting. This allows me to 'see' and 'hear' the stories of the past that are held within the fabric of our families, within the walls of buildings, places of purpose and the land itself. For me this all began at quite a young age. The nightmares began when I was twelve. Always the same. The fear...running...a faceless man...water...my death. I thought then it wasn't possible to dream of your death. I had read somewhere that you would wake yourself up before the nightmare got to that stage but this wasn't an ordinary nightmare.

My breath comes in ragged bursts and my feet start to drag through the sand. It becomes harder and harder to move forward and I am reduced to a crawl. My hands claw at the sand trying in vain to find a place of safety. The sobs come next with the knowing that there is no safe place. This is it, the end. Death is haunting me. It teases the skin on the back of my neck. I feel a sharp crack at the base of my skull and then the darkness comes. As I slip in to the darkness I feel the icy water begin to lap against my toes but the darkness is insistent and I can resist no longer. I slip under.

I would wake and sit up in bed, horrified at what I had just seen. The dreams became more vivid and insistent in their intensity. I eventually realised that the female I am seeing was not me. She felt like me, she looked like me but she was NOT me. This knowledge helped somewhat but the dream kept rolling just the same. After a while it didn't wait for sleep, it came in the day and there was no escape from it. I called it the 'black light'. That feeling that comes when the 'other world' is speaking to you. A tugging at my vision to look beyond, to listen to their words, to feel what they feel. I spent years blocking it out. As a teenager it floored me. I spent 18 months in bed, home from school practically comatose at the height of the nightmares and the black light. Until I listened. Until I learned how to flow from one world to the other, attempting to 'fit in' with both.

It was a number of years later that I became properly acquainted with the woman from my dream. Her name was Catherine and she was my great-grandmother. She drowned when my Mother was pregnant with me. In fact my Mother was on her way to see Catherine, to tell her the news of the pregnancy, when her body was found. Her body was found washed up on the beach. The story goes that she went for a walk on the beach, fell asleep in a cave and got caught by the tide. A tragic accidental drowning... This is not quite the story that Catherine tells. Hers is quite different.

My family is from a string of fishing villages in the Scottish Highlands. I am tied to that land. When I am there I can breathe, I am home. Whenever I go 'home' another piece of the story comes to me. After the birth of my son the dreams began again. This time she had my attention. I listened and I made a promise to tell her tale. So many secrets swept under the carpet. This is what drew me to Family Constellation work.

The things that have happened in the family in the past cannot be changed, but they have to be seen and accepted in order to move on, and the Ancestors can be acknowledged and allowed to rest in peace. This, in turn, allows us to move forward with peace in our heart.

Sit quietly... Think a while with me...

What is really going on inside of you?

What is your question?

What is your pain?

When I work with individuals now I use a combination of approaches to suit each individual client. I always spend time at the beginning looking at the 'why?' By doing this I am passing the responsibility for their decisions, their choices back to them. If they are fully present during a session and take responsibility to be present then the effects are far more beneficial than if I were to simply 'read' their energy and tell them what to do. The individual can then in turn fully participate and doesn't have to defend themselves against someone telling them how their life is.

Whilst they are either sitting pondering their truth or speaking it out loud, the reason that they are here, I sit opposite them connecting with their energy, tuning into their family energy, exploring the ancestral line. Sometimes I see the person connected to this knot or entanglement, or the person nearest to them who perpetuates this pattern. This entanglement can be something that has happened generations before that has been strengthened by more recent events within the family or in that particular aspect of the family line. I listen to the voices from the past and I look to see where everyone in the family is drawn, where the tangles and the knots are. As I look I take them all to my heart, they all have a place. My allegiance is with the ancestors and with the dead and I listen to their story.

The Origins of Family Constellation

Bert Hellinger is considered by many to be one of Europe's most innovative and provocative psychotherapists; he studied psychoanalysis, and eventually developed an interest in Gestalt Therapy and Transactional Analysis. It was in Hellinger's later training in family therapy that he first encountered the family constellations that have become the hallmark of his work. Hellinger's Family Constellation therapy is based on the principle that everyone within a family, known as the family system, is energetically connected within this family field by something that he calls the in-forming field.

When doing the constellation in a group setting, the individual will choose representatives from the group for each of the family members (sometimes the individual will choose a representative for themselves so that they can observe the full picture of their constellation before taking their own place). The individual then places the representatives in position to one another as a spatial representation of their emotional connection. The representatives are then asked to take note of how they are feeling emotionally, physically and how they respond to the other representatives. The constellator then moves the representatives, with continual feedback from them, searching for where the tension is held and where the point of resolution is.

When working with the family of origin, there can be an overwhelming array of connections and entanglements between family members which draws energy away from the family field.

It is important to hold focus on the most powerful of those and to bring it into balance for the individual concerned. With the present family the focus can be on giving former partners their place, easing the relationship between the two masculine and feminine roles and the children involved, as well as travelling through the generations bringing to light those that need to be seen. Ultimately we are looking for the point of balance that is comfortable for all the representatives and the individual in question.

Hellinger's work continually evolves and it is a joy to learn from him and the other teachers who have taken his work and moved forward with it in their own way. Hellinger's approach encompasses the essential elements of the present family or the impact of the previous generation on the family of origin. When working with a large or experienced group, deeper ancestral patterns often emerge that correlate with the more recent entanglements within the current generations and highlight effectively the root of the issues.

Setting up a constellation is like taking steps into the realm of the family, the realm of the ancestors and the realm of the dead whilst observing, understanding and feeling how one weaves in to the other drawing on the individual in question.

An individual constellation is very useful for someone who is uncomfortable with group working, if the issue is particularly sensitive, if there is a very specific issue that the client wants to work with or for practical reasons where a telephone consultation is the only option. When working with an individual it is possible to carry out the constellation either in their mind's eye, through a series of guided visualisation exercises or through using representatives of the family members. For individual work I use coloured squares for the representatives which are placed in the family field, by standing on each of the squares in turn I can begin to tune in to the field and we progress through the constellation together with the individual standing within the constellation.

With those individuals who have previously completed some personal work whether that is in a therapeutic or esoteric setting, the constellation can have a different feel and deeper ancestral connections that come through can be more prevalent. As we work through the layers of our being we tend to begin with our place within our family of origin and the dynamics of mother, father, siblings, we then move on to our relationships and loves and our own children. Then the deeper soul group and ancestral themes emerge.

It is important to remember that a family constellation is not a miracle cure for all. It gives a "new picture" for the individual or the family to move forward from, a clear reflection of how the situation actually is. This new picture has to be accepted into the heart otherwise the old patterns just keep playing on repeat. It is easy to sense when there is unwillingness on the client's behalf to see the situation as it really is, or to accept the changes or even their own role. At this point the constellation has to be stopped until such time that the individual is ready to move forward themselves. It is essentially in their hands. At times it can be overwhelming, so that even when the client can see the entanglement as it is there is an inner resistance or fear to step forward in to the new picture. The work must be done at the client's pace and if they need to step back and breathe for a while before slowly making their way forward then that is how it has to be. If a constellation is rushed or the facilitator pushes on to the end point without allowing the client to feel their way there themselves then it is of no use and can ultimately be damaging. There can be great resistance to seeing the family as it actually is.

My introduction into the existence of family constellation and ancestral patterns came from the world of tarot. When I work intuitively with people I see the patterns of their life and how they link in with their partner and their partner's patterns. How they link in with their ancestors and the parallels and resonances that are felt between partners and their respective ancestral fields fascinates me and I find it all unfolding around me as I look. I am pulled through the web of intimate connections and patterns with previous partners, with the children, with the siblings, the parents and the ancestral lines. I suspect that clients are often baffled as I point out the various parts of the web that I see surrounding them. We delve in to the family and deeper ancestral connections (at times almost tribal connections) together and then bring it back in to the intimate family connection. My passion, my fascination is to explore the present dynamics that particularly impact the children, involving the unseen, the missing and to see how the children can so clearly be drawn to the ancestors and their fates.

It is comforting to think of family members in terms of the role that they hold within the family without thinking of what their life was like before parenthood struck. With renewed interest in family tree hunting and ancestral research this is hopefully changing. A little scratch at the surface of the happy family veneer can be very revealing. A simple search into my own family tree revealed illegitimate children, loss of a first love during the war, rape, murder, early death of parents, an individual being excluded from the family and this was only looking at two generations of the family... What stories do your ancestors have to tell you? What secrets are waiting to be uncovered? Whose fate are you drawn to? Whose steps are you mirroring with your own?

Chapter Two

The Mother and the Female Line

When you start to think of all the ways in which you could be unconsciously echoing the past and carrying the burdens and fates of those that have gone before you, it can begin to feel a little overwhelming. Where on earth should you begin to look? Let us look at your family of origin, which is the family that you have grown up with. Your place within your family is influential in many different ways, from how you interact with your family to your openness within relationships with people outside of the family, such as friends, partners and colleagues. It is essential that you hold your own place within the family and that all around you is at peace. We begin by exploring this family of origin and look to see who is essentially missing. Who could possibly be missing from the family of origin? We look to the dynamic between the Mother, Father and siblings to find out.

Take a moment now.

Close your eyes and think of your Mother.

In your mind's eye see her standing before you.

Feel your connection to her.

Breathe in that moment.

How does it feel for you?

What comes in to your mind as you look upon your Mother?

Your relationship with your Mother, and the female line itself, is influential over many different aspects of your life. However it is often difficult to separate out your Mother, the woman, from the role that she embodies as your Mother. Seeing her only in this limited way can in itself limit our connection with our family, our sense of place, our relationships, our own children as well as our creativity.

Can you imagine your Mother as a child, growing up within her family with all the entanglements therein?

Can you imagine her hopes, her fears, her dreams?

See her in your mind's eye meeting your Father, beginning their relationship together.

Now look upon their combined hopes and dreams for the future, do they have to compromise or sacrifice for one another?

For their families?

Now see her in your mind's eye as she discovers she is pregnant with you, how does that feel?

Can you see the different directions in which she is pulled?

Her different loyalties and entanglements?

See or feel the sacrifice that is made as she is transformed from woman to mother, what price does she pay to be your Mother?

What price do you pay to be her child?

Go back to the beginning now...

Close your eyes again and think of your Mother.

In your mind's eye see her standing before you again.

Feel your connection to her once more.

Breathe in that moment...

How does it feel for you now?

The link to our ancestors and the roots of our being starts very close to home. It starts with our parents, they are the beginnings of our ancestral line and for many the relationship with their parents is the stumbling block or the root of the issue that holds them back in their life. Hellinger likens the Mother in some ways to be representative of a "spirit-mind" and therefore a rejection of the Mother is a rejection of life itself. To say that you want different parents, that they weren't good enough, and that you didn't receive enough from them is to say that you want a different life; your life isn't good enough, it is not enough for you. You cannot change your parents, they are who they are. Just as you cannot change who the Mother or Father of your children are. If this can be acknowledged with love then the children become free with nothing to hold them back in life, if this cannot be acknowledged or accepted as it is, then the children continue to perpetuate the same patterns within their life and pass them on to their own children. Their children will treat them as they treated their own parents. And so it goes on.

This sounds a simple idea when it is presented without any other dynamics or entanglements that may be at play within an individual's life, but this does not take away from the profound effect of simply acknowledging and honouring the Mother and the Father within Family and within society as a whole. For some the revelation of the sacrifices and energy required to be a parent cannot be fully comprehended until they themselves become a parent. The solution is to look to your roots, your own family. See your Mother (and your Father) as they actually are. You cannot change them, they are who they are and without them you would not have your life. Being able to accept your parents, your Mother and your Father and to give thanks for your life is to be able to accept yourself and take your place. When you can do this your children will follow.

Your mother is the person that brought you in to the world, alongside your Father she gave you your life. The natural order is for children to take from their parents that which their parents give with love. Your connection with your Mother and your ability to accept your life from her and the sacrifices made for you are influential on your ability to be successful in your relationships, friendships, career and creativity as well as your own parenting skills. The Mother's line is a line of divine creation and sacrifice. What is it to be a mother, that role? We find it difficult to see the woman, her entanglements to her own family, what she carries into being a mother, what she gives of herself. She represents your creativity, your love, your communication, everything...

We can be very hard on our Mother, measuring up our childhood to those around us and checking to see if we have received 'enough', making bold claims that we will do it differently with our own children.

Mother Interrupted

We spend a lot of time analysing the role of the Mother and looking for answers as to why things are the way they are and wishing that they were perhaps different. The following is an example from a group constellation workshop where a young female requested a constellation to explore her relationship with her deceased mother. She feels as if she has no connection to her Mother and experiences loneliness and difficulty showing emotions and being vulnerable in relationships. She feels as if she pushes people away from her and thinks it is connected with her relationship with her Mother. She chooses a woman from the group to represent her mother and places her standing across from her. The mother had committed suicide 18 years previously.

The two stand opposite one another for a long time. Chloe is looking at her Mother but the Mother's representative finds it hard to look at Chloe. Instead she looks to the floor, she shares

Figure 1 - Chloe and her Mother

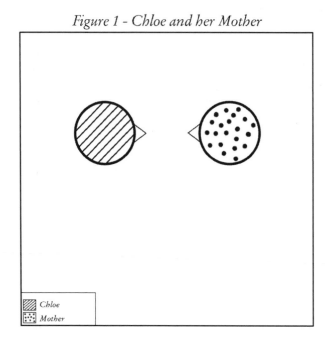

that she feels more peaceful when she looks at the floor and that it is "too much" to look at her daughter. The representative for the Mother begins to feel very weak. She begins to sway and finds it difficult to stand. She bends forward towards the floor and is clearly being pulled to the dead. Chloe becomes very distressed and tries to reach out to her Mother. I place a representative on the floor lying down in front of the mother. Both Mother and Daughter feel relieved by this and the Mother is able to look at her Daughter. Chloe say "I am here. I am your Daughter and you are my Mother". The Mother smiles at her but then begins to feel agitated and feels pulled downwards again. I place another representative lying down alongside the first. The Mother visibly relaxes and eventually lies down beside them saying to her daughter "This is my fate, I accept it." As she says the words she smiles in relief. Chloe also visibly relaxes though she expresses a wish that her mother was still with her. I ask her to look at her Mother and how relaxed and happy she has become. Then I ask

state. She then spent the next few years of her life in the guardianship of Gladys' best friend, Grace McKee. She was passed from her care, to an orphanage, to foster care and back again. During her time at the orphanage, several families were interested in adopting her; however, reluctance on Gladys' part to sign adoption papers thwarted those attempts and her unstable upbringing continued, peppered with allegations of sexual abuse. The final outcome being that a 16 year old Norma Jean ended up marrying a neighbour's son to avoid returning once more to an orphanage or foster care. In 1943 during World War II her husband enlisted in the Merchant Marine and was shipped out to the Pacific. It was during his time away that Norma Jeane was discovered and Marilyn Munro was born (Munro representing her mother's maiden name of Monroe).

Her career was characterised with rumours of difficult, hostile behaviour, health issues surrounding fertility and miscarriage, as well as reports of alcohol and prescription drug addiction. Her love life was tumultuous to say the least. Upon reading the family lines it is clear to me that there is a heavy fate associated with the men linked to the female line. By that I mean that I am drawn to a link with her Mother's Father and his family at that time. I believe at this point there is a strong break or fracture within the family that is possibly linked to a violent event. Munro's Mother is entangled with this. Her family field is further complicated with entanglements associated with the 'adoption' of Marilyn by her Mother's best friend. Generally speaking with adoption the child is firstly tied to the birth family and he/she carries the unresolved issues and family fates from that family into the adopted family. Issues can occur when the adoptive family try to erase or replace the birth parents. The child will generally always be tied to their birth Mother and Father, if instead the adoption occurs in such a way that the birth parents are acknowledged as coming 'first' with the adoptive family 'second' the child becomes free. Another factor to consider with adoption is often the anger or deep emotion the child feels at the separation from the Mother. A part of the child will always be waiting for the birth Mother to come back for them. In Munro's case this was further emphasised by the Mother's best friend's reluctance to allow her to become part of another family. She too was waiting or perhaps felt bound by an unconscious promise compounding Marilyn's sense of having no place. With this in mind it is not surprising to see the lifestyle choices the young Marilyn made as she was torn between the realms of the family and the realms of the dead. Within the constellation there is also a strong sense that there is a sibling missing before Marilyn that she is particularly pulled to. There is also very little connection or ability to 'see' her father or the male line, with this comes a very heavy feeling of guilt (that she carries but that does not belong with her). Someone who is entangled in this way will often unconsciously sabotage themselves in an effort to remain unseen as they attempt to sacrifice their place for the missing within their family system.

Figure 2 - Marilyn Monroe's Family Constellation

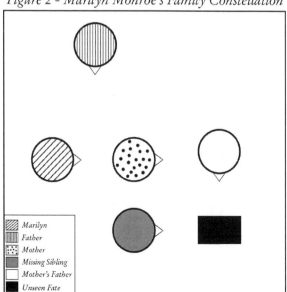

Monroe died on August 5, 1962, when she was 36 years old. Her cause of death was cited as "acute barbiturate poisoning," resulting from a "probable suicide".

Carrying the Burden

When children unconsciously take on the burdens that belong to their parents, or treat their parents as if they were the children, then it causes a great imbalance within the family field. During a group constellation a woman called Susan came forward and asked if we could explore together the relationship she had with her Mother who is an alcoholic. We set up the constellation including Susan, her younger sister, her Mother and her Father. Susan had promised her Father as he was dying in hospital that she would look after her Mother for him. The Father had suffered a long and protracted illness. He had been agitated throughout his stay in hospital and had hovered at death's door for quite some time. As soon as Susan spoke aloud her 'promise' to her

Figure 3 - Carrying the Burden (1) with Susan

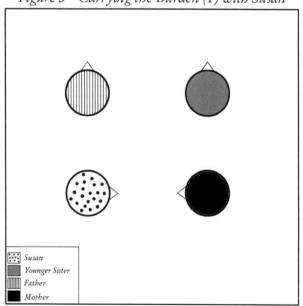

Susan
Younger Sister
Father
Mother

Father he quietly and peacefully passed away. From that point on the structure of the Susan's life gradually deteriorated. Her Mother's alcoholism had also worsened and she had begun stealing to fund her habit. Susan felt helpless in the face of the promise she had made to her Father and angry with her Mother.

The constellation that had been set up showed a family scattered by a specific fate. The Father had turned away and could not look at either his wife or his daughters. The younger sister had also turned away, refusing to acknowledge the other family members. Within the constellation Susan was finding it increasingly difficult to stand and her legs were visibly shaking. The Father could not look at her and moved further away, the younger sister also stepped further back. The Mother who stood opposite Susan laughed and the representative described the experience as feeling a little mad or crazy. I felt at this point that there was a heavy entanglement within the female line, an unacknowledged guilt; I placed a representative for the Mother's

Figure 4 - Carrying the Burden (2) with Susan

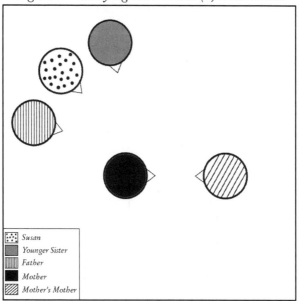

Susan
Younger Sister
Father
Mother
Mother's Mother

Mother within the constellation behind Susan's Mother.

The inclusion of the maternal grandmother had a strong impact on the family. The Father turned back round to face his family and was displaying anger towards his Mother-in-law. The Mother became somber, refusing at first to look to her own Mother. The representative explained that she felt she had 'shrunk' in size. Susan's legs stopped shaking, though she still felt weak and confused. After some time the Father moved to stand alongside his two daughters. Both Susan and her sister felt strength and support from their Father. After a while the Mother turned to face her mother. The two stood and looked at one another for a long time and then they both turned away, looking outwards together at their shared fate.

Figure 5 - Carrying the Burden (3) with Susan

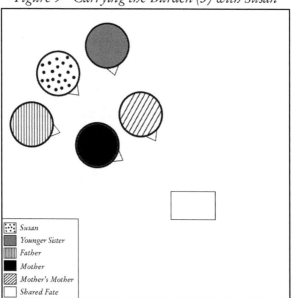

Susan was then able to let her go. She said to her Father "I cannot keep this promise for you, it is not mine to keep." To her mother she was able to accept the choice that her mother had made about her fate. She was then able to turn around from the family and step in to her future.

Acceptance

Our connection with our Mother and the Mother's line can be the storage point for the judgements, opinions and beliefs that we have about the world and ourselves and is also the storage place for our will and willpower. A rejection of our Mother or that line results in a weakening of this energy centre, affecting our ability to drive forward successfully in our life. If an individual cannot accept their Mother and essentially their life, they often disconnect from their roots and go off on various personal/ spiritual quests to find themselves.

When I am working with someone who struggles with their connection to their mother and the mother's line there is often a child like or even childish quality to their view of themselves and the situations that they find themselves in. It is as if they become 'stuck' in the energy of a child and are often resistant or unwilling to let go of what they hold within.

When we connect with our Mother the comfortable point that we aim to reach is to be able to see her as she really is. See and honour what she carries in terms of her place within the family and her connection to our Father and to be able to accept our life from her. If, when you are attempting to connect to your Mother through your mind's eye, you find it difficult to 'see' her or to physically experience the connection, or perhaps the image is blurry or not fully formed, then that is often an indication of her being caught up in an entanglement or family dynamic that pulls her away from the family system. As you include your Father and other family members and seeing the ways in which she is pulled, the connection with her should become clearer and more accessible.

Chapter Three

The Father and the Father's Line

Take another deep breath.

> Close your eyes and think now of your Father. In your mind's
> eye see him standing before you and take the time to really
> look and see him.

> Feel your connection to him, feel it in your heart.

> How does your connection to your Father feel for you?

The male line has a very different feel compared to that of the
female line and can often be easily overlooked. Have a think
about what it might feel like to change from boy to man to Father.
What sacrifices may be involved? What does the boy have to
leave behind to become a man? What price does one have to pay
to become a Father?

How would you define today's modern family? If you think of
a definition of the modern family, you would perhaps instinctively include a Mother, but would you also instinctively include
a Father?

The traditional role of the male in Western society has shifted
hugely over the last century. The feminist movement and the
search for equality for women have impacted all aspects of our
modern Western lives. Women now have a place alongside, and
in some cases in place of, their male counterparts. Is there any
real place where the role of the male is truly left standing tall? In
saying this I am in no way denigrating the emancipation of
women or the feminist movement. In the much needed push to

rebalance the feminine, the unique and valuable qualities and contributions of the masculine have, in my opinion, been somewhat devalued and rendered invisible. There is now a need to acknowledge value and respect the place of both the feminine and masculine roles within society and within our own individual families. In particular the role of the Father and the role of the Mother, both have an equal right to belong.

The vast majority of participants on my group constellation sessions are women. The issues they are drawn to are many and far reaching, but an underlying element of many aspects of the work is the dynamic between the masculine and the feminine. I have observed a great reluctance within some women to look to the Father's and the male line, and a great surprise at what they experience when they choose to look and connect. What they experience is the quiet sacrifice and sense of service that flows through the masculine line that often isn't seen or acknowledged. This reluctance to look to the men is extended to the dynamic between men and women in personal relationships. There is an inability to acknowledge the sacrifice of the male line and an inability to say 'Thank you'. There is something happening to the role of men or to the perception of the role of men. It is socially acceptable to be a single parent, it is socially acceptable to become a single mother, it is socially acceptable to be a working Mother, it is commonplace for women to work in fields that were previously thought of as "male dominated", it is also possible to become pregnant via artificial insemination. (In May 2008 in the UK MPs voted to remove the requirement that fertility clinics consider a child's need for a father).

I believe that the role of the Father is equally important to the role of the Mother. Both deserve and should hold an equal place in our hearts. When one is excluded, be it the Mother or the Father, it impacts on the children and the subsequent generations of children that follow. When a member of the family field is excluded, other members of the family, be it that generation or future generations, will unconsciously attempt to redress the balance. This 'attempt' can take many different forms, but the observations of people such as Bert Hellinger show that the effects can be far reaching and very serious. Eating disorders such as Bulimia and Anorexia can occur in young children where they are torn between their loyalties to their Mother and their Father (Bert Hellinger, Colleen Beaumont. To the Heart of the Matter: Brief Therapies Dec 2003). The absence or the exclusion of the Father will very often result in issues around addictive behaviour, whether that is smoking, alcoholism or drug abuse. Depression too is a strong indicator of the effect of missing males from the family. The incidences and occurrences of mental health issues such as depression and addictive, destructive behaviours such as alcoholism and drug addiction are also increasing. Major depression is the most common psychological disorder in the Western world (Seligman, M. E. P. (1990) *Learned Optimism*). It is growing in all age groups, in virtually every community, and the growth is seen most in the young, especially teens. At the current rate of increase, it will be the 2nd most disabling condition in the world by 2020, behind heart disease. Ten times more people suffer from major depression now than in 1945 (Seligman, M. E. P. In J. Buie (1988) *'Me' decades generate depression: individualism erodes commitment to others*. APA Monitor, 19, 18.) This increase is more prevalent in males than in females. [Leon, D A; McCambridge, J: *Liver cirrhosis mortality rates in Britain from 1950 to 2002: an analysis of routine data.*] I believe there is a common denominator throughout all of this and I don't believe that I am alone in my thoughts. There has been research investigating certain behavioural patterns within families, such as family histories of suicide, alcoholism and drug addiction. It is now well established that a family history of suicide indicates that an individual is at a raised risk for suicidal behaviour. In fact a family history of suicidal behaviour has been noted to be associated with suicidal behaviour at all stages of the life cycle, including those over 60, and across psychiatric diagnoses (reviewed in *Roy, Nielson, Rylander et al.,* 2000). This is also the case for those that self-harm and suffer from mood disorders, mental health issues or depression. "The development of alcoholism among individuals with a family history of alcoholism is about four to eight times more common than it is among individuals with no such family history," said William R. Lovallo, Director of the Behavioural Sciences Laboratories at the Veterans Affairs Medical Centre, Oklahoma City and corresponding author for the study. "Although the definition of 'family history' is different according to different researchers, we define it as when either or both of the person's parents have had an alcohol problem."(*William R. Lovallo et al.* May 2006.) Researchers in both fields of study (suicide and substance abuse) agree that there is scientific evidence that alcoholism/suicide/addiction has a family component, but the actual gene that may cause it has yet to be identified. Perhaps the pattern is not a genetic one but instead an ancestral one. Males are twice as likely as females to abuse or become dependent on substances except for the population of ages 12 to 17, when the abuse rates are nearly equal. The highest rate of substance abuse is in the age 18 to 25 population (*Addiction - Alcohol and Addiction Trends.* Reviewed in NASW Office of Social Work Specialty Practice Staff). According to the observations of Bert Hellinger in his constellation work, the incidents of depression, behavioural addictions such as alcoholism and drug abuse as well as suicide are linked to an event or pattern in the family, namely, when someone is missing or excluded from the family system (Bert Hellinger, Jutta Ten Herkel. *Insights: Lectures and Stories.* 1 Jan 2002). In the particular case of depression or addictive behaviours the missing or excluded person tends to be male or connected with the Father's line in the individual's family. Men are also more likely to be excluded by external factors such as work requirements and roles within society. The effect of war on

homeless again, literally without a place. I think it is quite clear that such an unstable childhood and upbringing would have a profound effect on an individual's self esteem. When I set up the constellation to explore the family dynamics, I found that there were missing siblings, Cobain did not seem to be the eldest child, there appeared to be one child before him that had either been miscarried or aborted (this is my opinion, based on what I experienced when I explored his family line). There was also particularly heavy fates within both the Mother's and the Father's family. Cobain was drawn however to his Father and the male line. The Father, within the setting of the family field, could not 'see' his children; instead he was drawn to the dead, victims of some violent trauma in my opinion, further back in the male line. This sort of entanglement often arises when living family members are pulled to the realms of the dead in an attempt to follow the dead or to 'give up' their place for them. Cobain felt simultaneously connected to the victims and the perpetrator which explains to some extent his fragile mental state and his propensity for addictive substances.

I find it really interesting that he was such a vocal opponent of sexism, racism and homophobia given the 'unseen' victims within his family line, this I believe, is related and would be his way of unconsciously giving them a voice. Throughout most of his life, Cobain is reported to have suffered from chronic bronchitis and intense physical pain due to an undiagnosed chronic stomach condition. He allegedly started using marijuana as young as 13. He has also been linked with use of LSD, heroin and alcohol. He was also reportedly diagnosed with attention deficit disorder as a child, and bipolar disorder as an adult (*Heavier Than Heaven: The Biography of Kurt Cobain*), which links in with missing siblings and the missing men and victims in the male line. There is a history of suicide, mental illness and alcoholism in the male line of the family which I believe is connected to the violent deaths and the victims within the line.

Where there is that type of fate within a family you will often find the generations that follow unconsciously are drawn to either the victims, or the perpetrators, or both, and instances of depression, aggression, substance abuse and suicide are common.

During the last years of his life, Cobain struggled with heroin addiction, illness and depression, his fame and public image, as well as the professional and lifelong personal pressures surrounding himself and his wife, musician Courtney Love. On April 8, 1994, Cobain was found dead at his home in Seattle, the victim of what was officially ruled a suicide by a self-inflicted shotgun wound to the head.

Figure 6 - Kurt Cobain Constellation

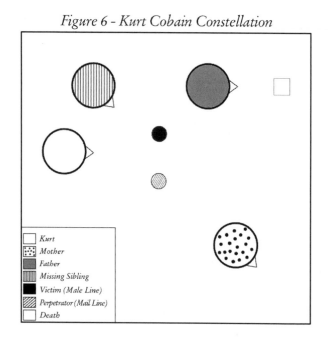

	Kurt
	Mother
	Father
	Missing Sibling
	Victim (Male Line)
	Perpetrator (Mail Line)
	Death

Fathers at War

Another interesting example of entanglements with the Father and the Father's line came to light during a one-to-one session with Aileen. Aileen had decided to come for a session as she wanted to explore the dynamics of her relationship with her daughter. She felt disconnected to her daughter and wanted to strengthen that connection now that her daughter was herself a mother. Aileen had never understood her daughter's career choices (she had joined the armed forces at a young age) or choice of home (she had moved from the UK and settled in Germany). Whilst Aileen was talking about her daughter I felt strongly pulled to her Father and the male line of the family. I decided to set up a constellation to explore her family of origin rather than the interplay with her daughter as I felt the root of the situation lay further back.

Figure 7 - Aileen Family at War (1)

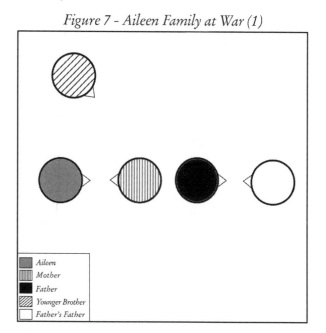

Included in the constellation were Aileen's younger brother, her Mother and her Father. The brother was extremely agitated and angry with the Father, whilst the Mother was attempting to stand between her children and their Father. Aileen was very drawn towards her Father. The Father was quite disconnected from the family and was turning away and looking behind him. I am aware of a strong war connection as I am looking at the constellation. When I ask Aileen about this she confirms that her

Father fought in World War II and her Grandfather fought in the World War I. I placed her paternal Grandfather within the constellation.

Figure 8 - Aileen Family at War (2)

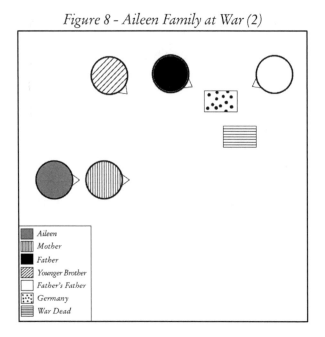

The inclusion of the paternal Grandfather provoked quite a strong reaction. Aileen became very agitated and felt great anger towards him, she couldn't look at him. The brother fell to the floor as did the Father. It was clear that they were being pulled to the dead, to unseen victims connected with the Grandfather and further compounded by victims linked to the Father. The Father was pulled to the victims and the dead, whereas the Grandfather, the true perpetrator, could not or would not see them. I placed representatives for victims of the two wars. The Grandfather still refused to look. I then placed a representative for Germany and it was only at this point that the field became more peaceful. By looking to his connection to that land, for him a land of sacrifice, he felt able to then see the victims as they actually were. We went on to do some further inner work to help Aileen come to a point of solution for herself and her family.

For Aileen this involved speaking directly with the victims and saying "You will always have a place in my heart. Please look on me with love as I stay" for her it was more comfortable to look at and to be with the victims rather than acknowledge her grandfather.

I then guided Aileen to see her Father in her mind's eye, connecting with him through her heart and saying to him: 'You are my Father & I am your Daughter. Thank you, I accept my life from you.' Then 'I can't carry this burden any more... I'm giving in back to you... Please Dad.' As she did this she sensed her Grandfather behind him. Only after completing this was she able to go in and look to see her connection with her Daughter. Her Daughter was tied to the Grandfather and his fate to the extreme of moving to Germany and working within the army.

I guided Aileen to see her Daughter standing before her, connecting with her through her heart, saying to her 'I am your mother and you are my daughter... This burden does not belong with you...you are the child here... It is time to let go.'

Accepting Yourself and Your Father

When children carry the burdens of those that go before them, they not only sacrifice themselves and their own place, but they prevent the dead from moving on and finding peace. The pattern is perpetuated. Our sense of belonging, desires, drive and ambition have strong connections with our Father and the Father's line. The roots of addictive behaviour and self-destructive patterns can also be found here as this is a link to the Father's ancestral lineage. When the Father (or other strong male from the masculine line) is missing, detached or rejected then this line is weakened. Our issues and burdens about ourselves and others are potentially linked to our emotional entanglements with the Male line. The solution is to look to the Male line with an open heart, to see the sacrifices therein and accept them, and then accept your own place in the line. It sounds so simple.

Dear Daddy

It can be hard to connect to the male line when there is a separation between the parents or if perhaps the origins of the Father isn't known to the child. In such cases the person in question can feel incomplete or feel a sense of loss in a particular area of their life. George came for a session as he felt he just couldn't settle. He was able to function in his working life but couldn't settle or find his place emotionally. His Mother didn't know much about his Father. They had met during World War II when his American Father was stationed at a base in England. His mother and father had shared a brief passionate affair and as a result his Mother became pregnant. She lost touch with his Father before she was able to share the news of the pregnancy with him. He was brought up by his mother in his maternal grandparent's home. I felt that his sense of restlessness and lack of emotional place was related to his lack of connection with his Father and his father's ancestors. When we set up the constellation he felt as though he couldn't connect with his Father, as though he kept disappearing. Instead of physically working through the constellation within the family field we decided to set it up instead in his mind's eye. He was able to feel a connection to and visualise very clearly his mother but felt just the absence of his father which distressed him greatly. I guided him through a visualisation where he connected with his Mother and how she felt upon meeting his Father. He was able to connect in with her feelings of love and excitement towards his father which in turn allowed him to create a representative of his father within his mind's eye. Interestingly he described his father as feeling emotionally withdrawn and isolated, feeling that he was pulling away from him and his mother which is very much in resonance with how George himself described his own emotional state.

When I asked George to bring in his Father's parents it again made the connection with his father feel more solid. When we also brought in an image to represent the war that separated his mother and father, George felt that his father turned round towards him and his mother at that point and he felt a connection with him in his heart. At this point in the exercise George visibly became more relaxed, his breathing deepened and slowed and his face showed expressions of relief. He said to his Father "Dad, I am here. I come from you too." at this point he began to cry with relief. He physically bowed down in acknowledgement of his father and the male line. The subsequent changes for George in his personal and emotional life have been quite incredible.

When an individual is able to acknowledge their roots from both their Mother and their Father there is a great sense of peace that can be felt in the soul. Taking this a step further and bowing down before the family and ancestors activates a level of connection, honouring and acceptance that allows previously entangled burdens to slip away. It is something more than words and it is a movement that begins in the heart and follows throughout the physical body that has deep emotional and spiritual reverberations. The conscious mind does not have a chance to step and stop the process. Something very deep can be moved within an individual when he bows down in front of his Mother/Father or the ancestral lines. It involves not only an acceptance of self and of life as it is but also the acceptance of the fates of the others within the family. Naturally there can be internal resistance to such an act, there is a vulnerability about the openness of it that is simply too great for some individuals depending on what has occurred within the family and at what stage the individual is at on their personal journey. It is interesting to feel and observe the physical response to someone resistant to honouring their place and their roots in this way. They tend to physically raise their head almost as a gesture of defiance and as they do so their posture and body become tense as they hold on to the energy and presumably the family entanglement within. If you try simply sitting in a straight back chair with your head and shoulders in a comfortable posture, breathing comfortably and naturally...and then raise your chin a centimetre or so upwards and feel the response in your physical body, the tension that is created there. Now imagine that physical response coupled with an emotional trigger or familial entanglement...there you see the effect of a simple physical bow and the potential for great change or for staying stuck and encumbered. What would you choose?

Some individuals such as George do not have a strong connection to their Father. They have no memories of their own to work through, they have no family stories to share and laugh about and there are no photographs to look at and identify with. If you don't know your Father or indeed your Mother and you don't feel connected to them within your heart then spend some time sitting in front of a mirror or looking at a photograph of your face. Study all your features, the colour and shape of your eyes, the curve of your mouth, the set of your jaw. Half of you is made up of your Mother and half of you is made up of your Father. Even if you don't personally know them or know exactly what they look like there are parts of you that do. There are parts of you that know them very well. If you, like George, know what your Mother looks like then spend some time looking at the features that are unlike them, that perhaps come from your father and his family. Feel the physical connection to them in that way. It is a step towards taking your place and seeing all of who you are. You can also look to and feel the connection to the ancestors beyond them. Those that were there and in existence before your own parents were even born. Their blood is your blood and sitting with the intention of connecting to them whilst being guided by your own heartbeat can be a revelation.

Chapter Four

Sibling Survival

Sisters and Brothers

Your place within your family is interwoven around your connection with and to your siblings. Your place within the 'order' of your siblings can and does influence various aspects of your life. In many ways this is recognised with the commonly accepted sibling stereotypes. We probably all have a preconception of the behavioural characteristics of the first born child, perhaps a conscientious, hard-working responsible type who doesn't stray too far from the accepted family conformity? The most gregarious and perhaps the most wayward in terms of digressing from the family structure would stereotypically be labeled towards the youngest. The middle child is often thought of as the 'difficult' one, unsure of their place in the family and resenting the youngest for being the new younger model, and irritated by the eldest's hand-me-downs. Lack of siblings doesn't mean that you escape a label, much is said of the 'spoilt only child' with common characteristics being described as selfish, lonely and a bit of a brat.

The first modern day psychologist to study birth order in any great depth was Alfred Adler, who formulated the theory of the inferiority complex in the 1920s. He believed that first-borns are loved and nurtured by their parents to the exclusion of all else until the arrival of the second child. At this point, the first-born is no longer the centre of attention, and has to contend with perceived feelings of rejection by the parents in favour of the younger sibling. Adler also suggested that eldest children are predisposed towards neuroticism and a deep seated sense of responsibility for those around them. This, in his opinion, is something that never leaves them and their greater likelihood to suffer from alcoholism and substance abuse can be attributed to this. He also believed that the youngest would be likely to be overindulged and spoiled, with this having a detrimental effect on social mannerisms and communication skills. In contrast he felt that middle children were somewhat immune to either of these experiences and would therefore have the best chance of growing up into successful, well-adjusted adults.

More recently there have been a number of studies suggesting that birth order is influential in terms of a person's material and financial success. And, contrary to Adler's conclusions about the psychological problems that come with being the eldest in the family, many have found that first-borns are more successful than those that come further down the sibling line.

Scientists at the University of Oslo used IQ tests taken from the military records of 241,310 conscripts and found that eldest siblings are, on average, significantly "more intelligent" than second-borns (2.3 points on the IQ scale is the average difference between first and second siblings).

Petter Kristensen of Oslo University also looked at second-born siblings who, because of the early death of their elder brother or sister, had become the eldest in the family at some point after their actual birth. What he found was that it was the actual role of being the eldest that was important. It was being reared as the eldest, rather than being born the eldest, that mattered, suggesting perhaps that the relation between birth order and IQ score is dependent on the social rank in the family and not necessarily just the birth order.

Another birth order critic is Judith Rich Harris, an American psychologist. Harris believes that the behaviors that children learn to use at home in order to 'fit in' with siblings are not the same as those they draw on outside of the home environment and in later life. "It was different in the old days. In former times, children spent most of the day in the company of their siblings, so a younger sibling might spend his entire childhood in the shadow of an older brother. And the rule of primogeniture meant that a child's birth order determined his status not only within his family but in the society as a whole," she says. "Yet people go on believing in the power of birth order."

She also discusses only children. Some researchers (Frank Sulloway) suggest that only children should be seen as intermediate personalities between the eldest and the youngest as they are not being pushed by a younger sibling into being particularly conscientious or aggressive, and they are not being pushed by an elder sibling into being particularly daring or unconventional. Sulloway's research also suggests that there are ecological "niches" in the family that siblings occupy, but that only children are free to occupy any niche.

According to Harris *"What Sulloway is trying to explain here is the embarrassing fact – embarrassing not just to him but to all believers in the nurture assumption – that only children do not differ in any systematic way from children with siblings...These children have missed out on the experiences that play such an important role in Sulloway's theory: they haven't had to compete with their siblings for parental attention, and they haven't had to learn how to get along (or not get along) with a bossy older sister or a pesky younger brother. And yet their personalities are indistinguishable from those of children with siblings."*

I find Harris' opinion on this really interesting, especially her comment on only children *"they haven't had to compete with their siblings for parental attention, and they haven't had to learn how to get along (or not get along) with a bossy older sister or a pesky younger brother."* I believe that in some cases this is exactly what has happened, particularly when you take on board the effect of missing siblings on a family system. Your place within your family in relation to your sibling line defines in many ways your place in life. Imagine now if you will, the effect of holding a place in your sibling line that does not belong to you. Imagine standing in the place of the eldest child, with all the expectation that goes along with it, when you are in fact the second or third child. 'Missing siblings' can have an impact on the surviving siblings in terms of their emotional communication with their living siblings, their parents and their ability to communicate effectively and succeed in the world outside of the family. By the term 'missing sibling' I refer to a child that is missing through a miscarriage, an abortion, a still birth or an untimely death. The missing children belong to the family, even if the miscarriage was in the very early stages of pregnancy and the Mother herself was unaware, and the energetic imprint of the child or children will still be there and their absence felt by the others.

Missing Siblings

The effect of missing siblings can be seen in the following example. I worked with Jessica in a Family Constellation group workshop. Jessica asked if we could set up a constellation to

Figure 9 - Jessica Missing Sibling Constellation (1)

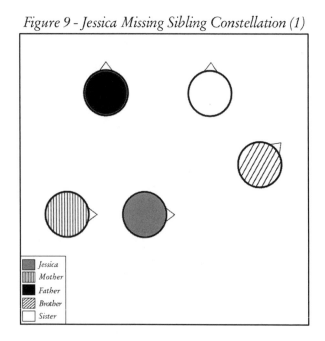

Jessica
Mother
Father
Brother
Sister

explore why she feels she doesn't fit in with her family. She described herself as feeling 'out of place' and 'as if she doesn't belong'. She is an American student living in the UK. She describes herself as feeling more at home in the UK as she feels comfortable within her invisibility here.

Jessica set up the constellation with her Mother, Father, Brother and Sister. Jessica is the eldest sibling, followed by her sister and her brother is the youngest.

During the initial set up Jessica placed her Mother behind her, hugging her. This instantly became uncomfortable and she had to move away. (This is an illustration of viewing a relationship as we would like it to be rather than seeing and feeling it as it actually is.) The representative for the Father is shivering and cold, he looks to the ground and can't look towards his wife or his children. The representative for the Mother says she feels cold and disconnected. It is clear that someone within the family is missing and that both the Mother and Father find it difficult to acknowledge this person. The three siblings are scattered and unable to look to one another, Jessica feels very emotional and the brother's representative says that he is experiencing a great sadness within his chest. I placed a representative for the missing family member within the constellation.

After some time the Father begins to turn round to look, however the Brother then starts to shake in a similar manner to the Father's previous behaviour. He cannot look to his fellow siblings or indeed his Mother. As well as the sadness he expressed earlier, he now begins to feel agitated. The new representative's legs begin to buckle and he falls to the floor. They are clearly representing the dead. The Mother is drawn towards the brother who is still shaking and feeling very weak but she feels helpless and she draws back. She cannot look to the dead family member, who is now lying on the floor, and she now cannot look towards her son. The sister is looking upwards at the ceiling, refusing to engage with her other family members; the represen-

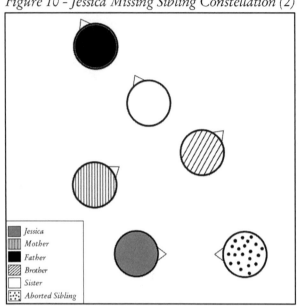

Figure 10 - Jessica Missing Sibling Constellation (2)

Jessica
Mother
Father
Brother
Sister
Aborted Sibling

tative describes it as feeling "in the clouds".

Jessica describes feeling sad and excluded. It is apparent to me that the representative on the floor is an aborted child, the true first child. I ask Jessica if this is the case and she explains that yes, her Mother had an abortion when she was a teenager.

The Mother cannot look to the aborted child on the floor. I physically move her round so that she is able to look. I ask the Mother's representative to look at the aborted child and to say "I can see you now" the Mother finds this very difficult to say, instead she slowly moves towards the aborted child until she is able to touch her. She then embraces her and says "I can see you now". The child's representative begins to cry. I ask the Mother to then say "I didn't want you then." As she says this, she visibly relaxes and describes a sense of relief. She can then go on to say:

"I can see you now."

They embrace together on the floor. The Mother and child look at one another for a long time and then she says:

"I take you as my child now"

"You can have me as your Mother".

After a while the aborted child sits up and leans back against the Mother. It is apparent that the Father of the aborted child is a previous partner of the Mother, this Father is placed within the constellation. The Mother looks to the Father and says "This is your child. I will bear this burden with you". Jessica feels particularly connected to and moved by this.

Figure 11- Jessica Missing Sibling Constellation (3)

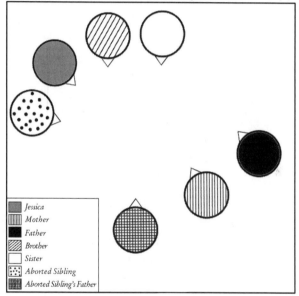

Jessica embraces the aborted child and says to them "You are the first and I am the second. We both have a place here".

The three surviving children and the first aborted child stand alongside one another. The parents move closer to one another. When the Mother sees the aborted child and can give him his place, taking him to her heart, then Jessica and the other siblings feel relief, they too can take their place.

In this situation Jessica was holding the place of the first child when she was in fact the second child. This can be a difficult position for a child to hold as they unconsciously sense the first child and attempt to acknowledge them, either by sabotaging themselves and their place in the family in order to essentially give up their place to the unseen child, or by perhaps attempting to achieve and live enough for the first child and themselves.

Abortion

I believe that there is little understanding of the effects of abortion on the family and it is generally viewed as a physical procedure with the spiritual and, to some extent, emotional effects not seen. I am not saying this from any point of judgement on the issue of abortion from either a pro-life or pro-choice stand point, I am only commenting on effects I have seen within constellations. It appears that when a child is aborted the relationship between the Father and Mother of the child often ends or irrevocably changes. The siblings before and after the abortion are also affected and if the Mother in particular cannot 'see' the aborted child, the surviving or subsequent children attempt to do this for her in an effort to bring peace to the family field. Part of the Mother also appears to 'die' with the aborted child and communication with any subsequent offspring is often hampered by this. It affects her ability to 'see' the rest of her family and will often also have a terminating effect on her creativity as well. In order to bring peace back to the family system, the aborted child must be seen by both the Mother and Father and given their place. The loss of children through miscarriage, at any stage, also draws part of the parent (the Mother in particular) to the realm of the dead. In turn her living children make some attempt to redress this for her. It is interesting to note here that individuals are more sensitive to those family members within the realm of the dead who aren't at peace when they themselves do not have their 'place' within the family system. A child who is holding the place of another is often more drawn to the fates of those that have gone before them.

Abortion and Siblings

Another of my clients, Margaret, came for a session as she was concerned with her 3 year old son's behaviour. She had recently split with her partner (the boy's Father) because of the partner's abusive behaviour towards her. She was refusing the father access to the son and was communicating with him via her mother-in-law. Her son's behaviour started to change; he gradually stopped eating and was withdrawn emotionally. We set up the constellation for the Son, Margaret and the Father.

Figure 12- Margaret Missing Sibling Constellation (1)

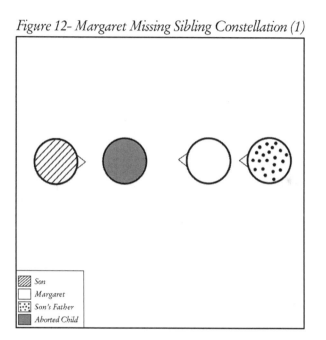

The Mother, Margaret, was standing in front of the Father blocking him from view of the son. The son's representative said that he felt invisible when he couldn't see his father; he then became distracted and withdrew from both his parents. He described a feeling of being pulled downwards. He was being drawn to the realm of the dead. He looked down to the dead and was distancing himself from both his Father and Mother. I placed a representative for the dead on the floor where the son was drawn to look. His representative described feeling less tense though he still refused to look to either parent and stayed with the dead. I asked Margaret if she had lost a child prior to the birth of her Son and she said yes, that she had had an abortion 5 years ago.

Figure 13 - Margaret Missing Sibling Constellation (2)

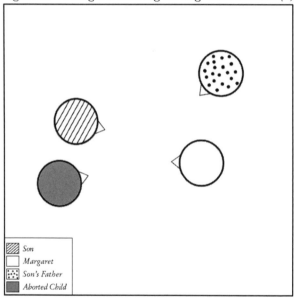

It was very challenging for Margaret to look and see the aborted child and to accept this child as hers. After a period of time she was able to look and then gradually move closer to both her children. Her Son was also able to step a little closer towards her and began to feel lighter in his heart, but he was still hesitant. I then asked Margaret to turn to her ex-partner and say:

"This is our Son, we will always share him. You will always be his Father and I will always be his Mother. Everything else that was between us has gone now but we will always share him".

When she said this the Father took a step to the side, away

from her but in line of sight of his son. The son's representative visibly relaxed when he heard his mother's words. Margaret then said to her son:

"This is your Father. I love that you are like him. There would have been another child, they are the first and you are the second."

The son at this point cries in relief and smiles at his mother and father.

When the mother could release her relationship to the husband, but still acknowledge him as the father, this drew the son closer. In time she also took the aborted child to her heart. A few days later the son started to eat. He had been entangled not only in the dynamic with the missing sibling but also, perhaps in part because as a result of this he was more vulnerable, in the entanglement that existed between his Mother and Father. When a break up between parents is difficult, the children suffer. Margaret's son was unconsciously rejecting the parts of himself that were like his father because he was torn between the two of them. He had lost part of his identity and his sense of place within the family system was affected. He felt in some way that it would be better if he disappeared. From this perspective he became aware of his aborted sibling and entangled further with their fate. A situation such as this can be at the root of eating disorders within children.

Jimi Hendrix and his Siblings

I find this work fascinating and am constantly intuiting my way through the family lines as I come in contact with people or read about their situations. I found myself absorbed when reading about the family background of Jimi Hendrix. Jimi Hendrix is considered to be the greatest electric guitarist in the history of rock music by other musicians, muso's and my husband, who brought the background of Hendrix's life to my attention. There are many interesting aspects to consider when you look at

Hendrix's formative years and family fates. He was born on November 27, 1942, in Seattle, Washington, while his Father was stationed at an Army base in Oklahoma. He was named Johnny Allen Hendrix at birth by his mother who is reported to have left him in the care of friends. When his Father was released from the Army he took him in and changed his name to James Marshall Hendrix to honour his deceased brother, Leon Marshall Hendrix. The Mother and Father then reunited for a period of time. At this point you can perhaps see that an abandonment of a child by the Mother so soon after birth and almost a deletion of his place in favour of representing a deceased family member would have an impact. However the dynamics at play are further complicated by his relationships to his siblings. Hendrix had two younger brothers, Leon and Joseph, and two younger sisters, Kathy and Pamela. The three younger children Joseph, Kathy and Pamela were all born with physical difficulties. Joseph was given up and placed in to care at the age of three. His two sisters were also both given away and placed in care at a relatively early age, and were later adopted.

On looking at the specific patterns presented and feeling my way through the family lines, it would appear that there is a particularly heavy fate within the Mother's line (Lucille) that both Jimi and the three physically disabled children are drawn to. In fact they are attempting to carry this burden for her. Leon instead looks to his Father's fate. It seems as if the Mother is herself carrying a burden from further down the line that her Mother was unable to carry and this affects her ability to 'Mother' her own children. When she 'sees' her children carrying her fate for her in such a clear way it becomes too much for her to bear and she gives them away. Hendrix's parents divorced when he was nine years old and his mother, who had cirrhosis of the liver, died when he was a teenager. He had little stability in his home life and was sent to live with other family members and his brother Leon was put into temporary welfare care for a period. Her addictive behaviour and abandonment of her children combined with the 'fate' within the family suggests to me that there is a strong pattern of violence within his mother's family line combined with the absence of significant male figures. Much has been written of drug use and abuse by Jimi Hendrix and in part you can relate this to his sabotaging of self and guilt at having his place and being 'seen' compared to the fates of his siblings. Hendrix died in unclear circumstances on September 18, 1970 in London. It can be difficult for children when one of their siblings has a physical disability. There can be tremendous guilt at accepting your own place and living your life fully. The solution is to bow to the fate of the other sibling and accept them as they are, accepting your own life alongside theirs. You both have a right to belong and to be at one with your particular fate. This can be particularly difficult to accept for some.

Van Gogh's Place

Growing up I was fascinated by the impressionist painters Monet, Manet and Vincent Van Gogh. I remember learning of Van Gogh's emotionally tortured existence, decline into madness and his suicide and so was really very curious to learn some more about him. Vincent Willem van Gogh (born 30 March 1853), a Dutch Post-Impressionist painter, suffered from extreme anxiety and increasingly frequent bouts of mental illness throughout his life, and died at the age of 37, from a self-inflicted gunshot wound. He is widely regarded as one of history's greatest painters and an important contributor to the foundations of modern art. Little appreciated during his lifetime, his fame grew in the years after his death.

He was the son of Anna Cornelia Carbentus and Theodorus van Gogh, a minister of the Dutch Reformed Church. Vincent was given the same name as his grandfather — and a first brother stillborn exactly one year before. This practice of reusing a name in this way was not uncommon but can lead to quite

Chapter Five

Love and Relationships

We are more likely to define who we are in terms of the relationship we are in or by the absence of an intimate relationship rather than through our family. I don't know if I have a particular draw to relationship patterns revealed within constellation because of my intuitive work, but I find the patterns and interplay between family and ancestral entanglements and intimate relationship patterns utterly absorbing. You can see the weaving of the web of the ancestors and the correlations that exist between a couple and their respective ancestral experiences, which in part seem to be an aspect of the unconscious attraction between individuals. There will often be similar ancestral fates. However they can be mirrored. So for example, where in the fourth generation back in an individual's family there will perhaps be unacknowledged victims of trauma, with the partner in the fourth generation there will perhaps be unacknowledged perpetration of trauma. This hidden dynamic moulds their relationship and communication with one another and yet is subject also to influence from previous partners they have both been involved with. Fascinating stuff! Patterns and entanglements from previous relationships can take many forms, but some of the most common involve the experience of a string of short or long term monogamous relationships that end within a similar length of time. Being unable to commit within a relationship, perhaps when a certain point in the relationship is reached, the urge to end the connection becomes irresistible. Oftentimes the repetitive occurrence of betrayal, lack of commitment, or dominating partners will flag up entanglements within the family system. Other indicators include an inability to 'let go' of emotions connected to previous partners. This can be highlighted and further complicated by difficulty in communication within any subsequent relationships. Difficulty seeing, connecting or communicating with a partner can perhaps suggest that either you or your partner are entangled with a previous love or fate and I see this so often when someone wants an appointment purely to explore my intuitive take on their current relationship communication issue. Experiencing difficulty communicating and connecting with your children often indicates a tie to a previous relationship where the children are unconsciously drawn to either the previous partner or the ancestors. In this instance your connection to your children (as well as your new partner) is 'blocked' by the link to the past where you and in some cases your off-spring are 'seeing' them rather than those around you.

Love, romance and relationships are generally at the forefront of our thoughts, if not our lives. The search for true love and our perfect partner can be all consuming. Great emphasis is also placed on maintaining the perfect relationship and what the 'behaviour' within a relationship should be. If we are not in a relationship then the media has much advice on rectifying this and to all intents and purposes who we are with (or not with) can ultimately define who we are as individuals. As I mentioned in chapter two the masculine and feminine roles have changed greatly over the last four or five decades and with that, the structure of intimate relationships has also changed. As the order and structure of the traditional family unit has changed so too have relationship 'rules' but there is much more to the dynamics of love than that...

My intuitive work with individuals really paved the way for me in terms of the work I now do with family constellation and ancestral patterns. The majority of individuals that came to see me were looking for guidance about love and relationships. Whether they were in a relationship, entangled with a previous love or looking to see if there was perhaps someone on the horizon, they all carried a similar thread. When working with them I could observe the influence of the patterns they carried with them throughout their life. This included ties to previous partners as well as familial entanglements. I also observed occasions where the individual became entangled with the partner's family to the exclusion of their own.

There is a fascination in observing the details and dynamics of other people's lives, their relationships, and comparing their fate to our own. In the case of celebrities, their lives are often splashed across the media with details of their everyday life examined for clues to explain the 'why?' of the situation. Why would someone cheat on a beautiful wife and children? Why would someone risk so much? What attracted them to one another? I don't believe the answers always lie within the relationship, I believe that the answer often comes from outside of the relationship. If a friend asked you to describe your relationship history, or for details about your current relationship, what would you say? Perhaps you would discuss the traits and idiosyncrasies of your partner, or possibly express regret or relief at the demise of a previous relationship. Perhaps you see your relationship being defined by your children. Would you think about the parental and familial influences on your relationship? Would you think about previous relationships as having an impact?

When we make an emotional bond to somebody through a committed relationship, an engagement or a marriage, we create a bond that cannot be broken. This bond is even stronger when a couple has a child together. When a relationship ends, any unfinished business or unacknowledged entanglements from the relationship are carried forward to subsequent relationships, and very often the events or entanglements repeat themselves. This doesn't just apply to your own relationship history, whatever that may be, it also applies to the generations before you, particularly if either of your parents had a significant prior relationship that didn't end well or has never been acknowledged. In this case, the children that are a result of the subsequent relationship are often 'tied' to the previous partner, seemingly forever fated to repeat that relationship dynamic, be it one of betrayal, lack of commitment, or of being 'unseen' within the relationship dynamic.

The dynamics of the entanglements within intimate relationships from a constellation perspective are fascinating. Not only is there an influence from the family of the individual concerned but also the partner's family and all the previous partners of both the individual in question and their current partner, with the dynamics becoming entangled further with each successive relationship. There is often resistance to the concept of honouring previous partners. However this is hugely important as doing so allows you to move forward and create space for the sort of relationship you truly desire. The emotional investment and entanglement created with a first love can be quite simply overwhelming but where does all that emotion go when the relationship ends?

Take a moment now and cast your mind back to your first love, your first serious relationship...

Remember how you felt when you first met and fell in love... The promises you made to one another...

The plans for the future you made together...

Now remember how you felt when it ended...

Though time may pass and you may move on, the tie to the person and the emotions experienced deep within still remain.

When you are exploring the dynamics of love within a constellation setting you are looking not only at the influence of one partner upon the other but also of the effect and entanglements of the previous partners as well as, very importantly, the patterns that exist within the family lines for the couple or individual in question. Not only are individuals influenced by the relationship pattern of their parents but often the secrets of fates that lie hidden within the family draw them in and influence their choice of partner too. So that if there is a fate within the family field that the family as a whole cannot look at or perhaps refuses to acknowledge, then the individual will be drawn to exclude themselves from their family of origin and effectively align and root themselves within their partner's family. In doing so they are in effect aligning themselves with their family's unseen fate and sacrificing themselves to that fate. They will often find themselves attracted to a partner whose family also carries a similarly heavy fate or burden. It is almost as if the price that they pay for their new 'place' within their partner's family is to 'see' the fate that exists within that family where the family of the partner cannot. Thus the one in the relationship that loves the most will carry the fate of the other. And so it goes on down the line.

Betrayal

Trust within relationships is sacred. When it is broken the dynamics of a relationship are changed forever. Looking in from the outside, we can be quick to judge betrayals of trust, and lay the blame at the feet of the one who has strayed, while viewing the spouse as an innocent victim. Perhaps we wonder what happened within the relationship to make those concerned behave in such a way. Often when you look you will find patterns of betrayed relationships within the family dynamic as well as within the relationship experiences of the individual in question.

If there is anything unresolved from the first significant

relationship then it will be carried in to any subsequent relationships. Unresolved issues can vary from lack of acknowledgement of the partner during the breakup of the relationship, to issues of betrayal, and difficulty in communication within the relationship as well as during the break up period. Even if you yourself feel 'fine' and that all is well or that perhaps the relationship wasn't particularly meaningful or important, the other individual involved may not be in agreement with you. Have you ever been spurned or rejected by a partner? How upset did you feel? Were you angry? Further down the line when you had both moved on, perhaps you found out that they had a new love, a new family…how did that make you feel? Now I want you to flip that round in your head and imagine perhaps what your previous partners are feeling or thinking when they think about you and your relationship… This is part of the reason why relationship entanglements and constellations are so complicated and why the dynamics revealed can be surprising and challenging. Not only do we explore your place and your experiences but also all of those people connected to you, past and present, as well as your family. Can you imagine the effect of a previous love's emotions of anger and resentment fixated on you and your new family? Can you perhaps see that this may create some obstacles for you and yours on your path forward?

Subsequent relationships will never be as close as the first or indeed any previous relationships until the first and those that follow are given their place. If the partner from the first relationship is not acknowledged, the subsequent partners will experience isolation within their relationship and most importantly the children from the subsequent relationship will be unconsciously tied to the previous partner. If the parent cannot acknowledge someone with the family field then the child will do so on their behalf. In this case if the parent cannot acknowledge the first partner the child will then take on the burden of this for the parent with destructive consequences.

Diana Spencer

The romantic and intimate life of the Princess of Wales, Diana Spencer, has been explored at length within the media with great focus on the alleged affairs within the marriage of the royal couple and Diana's subsequent relationships. I believe that the root of the relationship experiences can be found within the family of origin rather than within the relationship between Prince Charles and Diana. Diana was the youngest daughter of John Spencer, Viscount Althorp (later the 8th Earl Spencer) who was of British descent and Frances Spencer, Viscountess Althorp (formerly the Honourable Frances Burke Roche, and later Frances Shand Kydd). Diana was born in England on 1 July 1961. She was the fourth child to the couple, with older sisters Sarah (born 19 March 1955) and Jane (born 11 February 1957), as well as an infant brother, The Honourable John Spencer (born and died on 12 January 1960). The heir to the Spencer titles and estates, her younger brother, Charles, was born three years after her on 20 May 1964.

Her parents' had an acrimonious divorce in 1969 (over Lady Althorp's affair with wallpaper heir Peter Shand Kydd), Diana's mother took her and her younger brother to live in an apartment in London's Knightsbridge, where Diana attended a local day school. Every Christmas, the Spencer children returned to Norfolk with their mother, and Lord Althorp subsequently refused to allow them to return to London. Lady Althorp sued for custody, but her mother's testimony during the trial against her contributed to the court awarding custody of Diana and her brother to their father. On 14 July 1976, Lord Spencer married Raine, Countess of Dartmouth after he was named as the "other party" in the Dartmouths' divorce. Diana, like her siblings, did not get along with her stepmother.

Upon setting up the constellation to explore the dynamics within Diana's family of origin it becomes clear that Diana is strongly linked to a fate within the male line that involves her father and her deceased older brother. She is also pulled down quite strongly towards the realm of the dead. My impression is that the individual she is drawn to in the realm of the dead is a link to a war related death or violent occurrence (both her father and paternal grandfather served in war time) where the death was not able to be acknowledged or honoured in an appropriate way. I feel that the root of the fate is an entanglement with the Grandfather and that the burden of the fate has passed to the father, to the elder brother and subsequently to Diana. Where there are unacknowledged victims in the field in this way and when this is coupled with a 'missing' sibling, there can be a strong entanglement resulting in someone sabotaging or sacrificing themselves in a futile attempt to redress the balance of the unseen victims within their family lineage. In many ways it is easier to associate with the victims than with their own family. This possibly would contribute to the great drive Diana had for charity work which led to her unofficial title of "The Princess of Hearts". In terms of the relationship dynamics at play, there is also a strong pull within Diana towards a previous partner or love of the father whom she 'sees' more clearly and has a stronger connection to than that of her mother. The relationship between the father and the previous partner feels that it involves a betrayal and also feels that it was ended because someone who was perhaps a better 'fit' in terms of standing or status came along for the father. (This relationship would be prior to his relationship with Diana's Mother, Frances.) As the effects of this flow down the line, Diana then represents the betrayed and overlooked lover and is drawn to unconsciously repeat the pattern within her own life. We can perhaps see the effects of this played out in Diana's relationship with Prince Charles and his relationship with Camilla Parker Bowles.

Ancestral Patterns of Love

In my work I have observed some patterns that frequently occur when relationship dynamics and entanglements are explored. Patterns of betrayal, going through a series of long or short term relationships of a similar theme and abusive relationships can often have roots that lie within the family fates. Whereas patterns of lack of commitment or difficulty with communication tends to arise because of unacknowledged relationships within the individuals relationship history, though this too can of course be affected by family entanglements as well.

Laura – Illicit Love and Ancestral Betrayal

Laura has come for a session to explore her relationship patterns. She is a single mother with a 6 year old daughter. When she became pregnant with her daughter she made the decision to end the relationship with her partner without telling him that she was pregnant. She has had no subsequent contact with the gentleman in question and the daughter has never met her father. Since this time she has had a string of short term relationships which she describes as being shallow and without meaning. In order to explore the root of her relationship patterns we set up a constellation to include Laura, the father of her daughter and their daughter. There was an obvious dynamic created by the lack of connection between the daughter and her father and the non-acknowledgment of the Father's place which we worked through and at this point the daughter became more relaxed and comfortable with the addition of the father. She (the daughter) described the feeling as if she become 'whole' and was aware more of her feet and felt physically more present within the room, the acknowledgement of the father by the mother (Laura) lessened the anger that the father's representative had been displaying towards Laura though Laura herself still remained agitated. I asked Laura if there were any previous partners to be included within the constellation and she said no. At that point I decided to look to her family of origin and to explore the dynamics at play there. We added her Father and

Mother to the constellation. Laura immediately felt heaviness in her chest and her state of agitation increased. The Father became more and more uncomfortable and began to withdraw from his wife focusing instead on Laura. I placed an additional person within the constellation to represent a previous partner of Laura's father. Laura and the previous partner's representative became fixated upon one another. Laura felt pulled towards her and also experienced a feeling of deep sadness and pain. The Father could not look at either of them and became quite agitated. The constellation shifted at this point and it became clear that there was an entanglement between the father and the previous partner that remained unresolved. Laura had been unconsciously representing this woman for her father within their family. Laura got back in touch after her session to let me know some information that had come to light for her. She had made enquiries within the family as to who this first love for her father had been. A great aunt was able to tell her that her father (whose family were catholic) had fallen in love with a protestant girl. They had secretly become engaged and were planning to elope and marry. The girl became pregnant and the father's brother found out about the pregnancy and the planned elopement. Tragically the family responded with violence and three of the brothers were dispatched to "teach the pair a lesson." This resulted in a severe physical beating of Laura's father and his fiancée miscarried and lost their child. Laura had been unconsciously representing this woman for her father within the family to the point that she had isolated herself from serious relationships for fear of what they would bring and she also kept her child's existence a secret from her child's father and his family out of an unconscious fear of what may happen should they discover the child's existence. The solution for Laura was to give her father's first love a place within the family field and to deeply acknowledge the sacrifice that was made by her and her unborn child.

Marianne – I am better for you

Marianne originally came for a session to explore her relationship with her Mother. She felt that they had switched roles and that she in fact held the role of the parent whilst her mother became the child. Through the course of the sessions we discovered that this 'mothering' role was something that she adopted within other strong relationships in her life, including her relationship with her husband. She was extremely frustrated in both her relationship with her mother and husband and treated them in a very childlike way. The relationship you hold with your mother does in many ways set the tone for the other emotional relationships in your life as does your ability to accept your mother exactly as she is. If you cannot accept your mother (or your father) then you cannot fully take your own place in your life and the people that are attracted to you and that you form relationships with will be in resonance with this chosen 'fate'. We explored these dynamics further in a constellation with

Figure 14 - I Am Better For You (1)

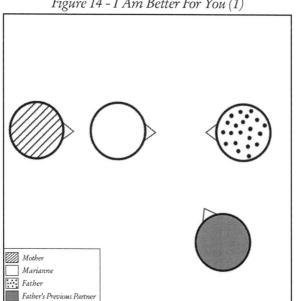

Mother

Marianne

Father

Father's Previous Partner

Marianne and her Mother and Father (who died when Marianne was 20 years old). Marianne set the constellation up with herself standing between her mother and father with her back to her mother facing towards her father. She was in effect blocking her mother from her father's view and felt energetically 'bigger' and superior to her mother.

I asked Marianne to say to her Father "I am better for you than her" when she said the words she laughed and said "Yes! This feels true!". These are however not the words of a child and they resonated for her because she carried the fate and the burden of another. When I asked Marianne if her father had been in a previous relationship, she explained that her father had actually been engaged when he met her mother and had broken off the engagement to be with Marianne's mother. I placed a representative of the father's ex-fiancée within the constellation.

Figure 14 - I Am Better For You (1)

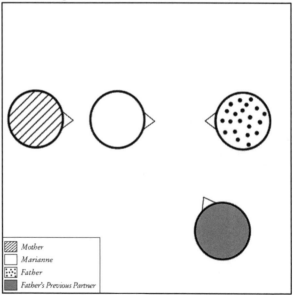

At this point Marianne was able to focus on her mother and see her for the first time. She felt confused as she looked towards the representative for the ex-fiancée. The representative for the ex-fiancée described herself as feeling great anger towards the father and felt proprietarily drawn towards Marianne. I asked Marianne to look at the ex-fiancée and say "You are important for me."

At this point Marianne visibly relaxed and smiled, she then said:

"You were the first and my Mother is the second. But she is my mother."

At this Marianne stood up a little straighter and said she felt a little bit of relief. I then asked her to say:

"I cannot keep this promise for you. Please let me go."

(The promise being the unconscious tie that she had to honour this previous relationship.) During this the ex-fiancée described a warm sensation at her heart and her anger became less intense. She was able to smile at Marianne and felt a great warmth towards her. The representative for the father then looked to the ex-fiancée and said

"You have a place in my heart but this is my family now... Please let us go."

The ex-fiancée said at this point that she didn't feel that she needed to stay any longer and withdrew from the immediate constellation. The mother was then able to step closer to her husband and daughter whereas previously she had been uncertain and afraid about doing so.

Within this constellation it was interesting to see that the reason Marianne could not accept her mother was because she carried the anger of the first fiancée of her Father. She took on the role of this previous partner and in doing so an internal movement was made in which she decided "I am better for you than her" when she looked to her parent's relationship. In doing this she fully took on the "Mother" role and this extrapolated out to her other relationships, including the relationship with her husband. Interestingly her husband has a stilted relationship with his own Mother and when we explored the relationship between the two of them through a constellation, Marianne had taken on the role of his Mother again with the inner movement "I am better for you than her". This in turn had affected the relationship her husband experienced with their children. When Marianne could look to her husband's family and accept him and them exactly as they were, saying "yes" to all of it, then they were able to move forward together.

I Will Save You

When there is a particularly heavy fate in the family that the family cannot look at, acknowledge or 'see' then it can be the case that an individual will form a romantic relationship with someone who has a similarly heavy fate. In this way, the individual can then 'see' the fate within their partner's family and tie themselves to that fate. They are in effect saving their partner and sacrificing themselves. If you think of a well known 'serial monogamist' you will most likely discover this pattern.

Julie came to see me to explore relationship patterns which she felt were destructive. She felt that she always picked people who were 'bad' for her. We set up a constellation exploring the different loves that have been important within her life. Her first serious relationship occurred when she was 17. She describes it as being very intense and says no other relationship has felt as intimate or emotional since. Julie's father died when she was 17 and she has never fully accepted this or been able to let him go; she describes it as feeling as if part of her died when he did. She wants to go to him and to be with him in the realm of the dead. She has had a series of destructive and abusive relationships since her first love when she was 17, with whose fate she is also entangled. She is sacrificing herself in the relationships that she has with men by being attracted to males with a similarly heavy fate and saying unconsciously 'I'll go instead of you, rather me than you,' making an emotional contract to carry their burden, as if she manages to sacrifice herself she will be able to give up her place and go to her beloved father. If she could look to and accept her life from her father this would free her. For Julie the path forward was to be able to accept and acknowledge the death of her father and say:

'Even though you've gone I'll stay.'

'I'm doing something special with my life to honour you.'

'My life is of value.'

When she does this she is able to accept the fate of her father and let him go in to his death and be at peace. She also shifts the dynamic of the heavy fate within her life that resonates with others who have a heavy fate. She is no longer on 'self-destruct' and sacrifice mode and is able to create a space for love within her life.

Jack Nicholson Constellation

Someone who has the media image of something of a ladies' man and a bit of a philanderer is Jack Nicholson. He was born in St. Vincent's Hospital in New York City, the son of a showgirl, June Frances Nicholson. June had married Italian American showman Donald Furcillo six months earlier in Elkton, Maryland, on October 16, 1936. However, Furcillo was already married and, although he offered to take care of the child, June's mother apparently insisted that she bring up her daughter's baby. Nicholson was brought up believing that his grandparents were his parents. Nicholson only discovered that his "parents" were actually his grandparents and his sister was in fact his mother in 1974, after a journalist for Time magazine who was doing a feature on Nicholson informed him of the fact. By this time, both his mother and grandmother had died (in 1963 and 1970 respectively). There is some controversy over whether Furcillo is actually the father and Nicholson has stated he does not know who his father is, saying "Only Ethel and June knew and they never told anybody", and has chosen not to have a DNA test or to pursue the matter. He has been romantically linked to numerous actresses and models throughout his life. When I explored the family dynamics present between Nicholson and his mother and father it was interesting to note that is was the fates within the father's line that Nicholson was most drawn to, despite the heavier entanglement that appeared to be present within the female line through the mother. Nicholson's energy and presence felt very 'big,' as though he was carrying the role of the parent as he looked to his own parents within the constellation. An individual will often appear 'bigger' when they carry a large fate for the family. In relation to his link to his father and the male line, he has a very strong pull and connection towards the previous partners of his father (it felt that there was more that one though the pull to the first was the strongest). So whether or not Furcillo is the father, it would appear that there were unresolved entanglements with the previous partners and that Nicholson is drawn in to representing that within the family, in a way he is saying "I am better for you than him" and this very much coincides with his apparent relationship choices and behaviours.

Maureen - Divorce

Maureen wanted to explore the dynamic between herself and her now ex-husband. He had chosen to end their relationship very suddenly after 20 years of marriage and shared business ventures. He was now refusing all contact with her and she felt that her (now adult) sons were being affected by this in their own life choices.

We set up the constellation with the wife, husband and the two sons. Immediately the representative for the husband became agitated and could not stand to look at his family. The eldest son started to withdraw from the others and the youngest son began to feel weak and experienced difficulty standing. The Mother was very confused and upset and didn't know where to

Figure 16 - Dynamics of Divorce (1)

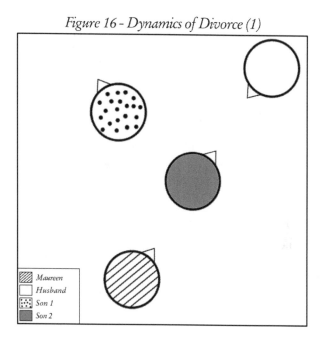

Maureen
Husband
Son 1
Son 2

place herself within the constellation, she was restless and uneasy.

I had a thought as I looked at the constellation about the fates that were affecting the husband and following this instinct I placed a representative for death behind the Father. He immediately calmed down and turned to look at death. Eventually the Father embraced the representative for death, laughing. The oldest son became very agitated saying that he would go in place of his father at this point and attempted to grapple with the representative for death so that he would release his father. At this point it was revealed that the Father, during an emotional breakdown some years earlier, when his son was a young child, had attempted to take his son's life.

The Father said to the representative for death "I accept my fate" and then "You and I belong together". This brings a great seriousness to the father though the two sons are still quite anxious and agitated. It is clear at this point that although this

Figure 17 - Dynamics of Divorce (2)

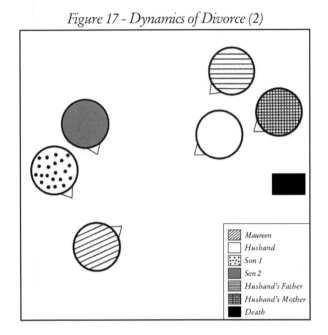

Maureen
Husband
Son 1
Son 2
Husband's Father
Husband's Mother
Death

representative was placed as 'death' he in fact represents a heavier fate from within the family. When representatives for the husband's parents are placed behind the husband, he feels much relieved and the inclusion of the Father's parents also allows 'death' to take a step back. Once the husband's parents (in particular his father) can look upon and acknowledge 'death' then 'death' is able to take a step further back again and smile upon the husband who says he feels as if a great weight has been lifted from him.

The Mother then looks to her sons and says:

"I am your Mother and this is your Father."
"In spite of everything I will always be your Mother and he will always be your Father."
"I love how much of your Father I can see in you."

The sons visibly strengthen and stand up. They are able to take their place. When one or other of the parents attempts to shield or protect their children from the other parent then the children are drawn unconsciously to the excluded parent and will often bear their fate/burden/behaviours out of loyalty to the excluded parent. When however, as above, the Mother in this example can give the Father his place and also cherish the Father within the children then the children in turn can draw strength from both parents and are often freed from the family fates. They also can accept all of themselves. Maureen was also able to honour the relationship with her ex-husband by saying to him:

> "You will always be important to me and have a place in my heart."
> "We will always share our boys...but everything else between us has gone."
> "I am ready to let you go now, please let me go too...and leave space for another."

When we can honour and acknowledge our previous relationships and give them their place, then we become free to move forward. If we cannot do this then there is no space for a new love to grow. What will instead come in will very likely be a repeat of previous experiences and a pattern is perpetuated. When each person that we have loved and been loved by is given their place in our hearts and when we are able to see in them what we saw in the beginning, what we fell in love with and separate with the memory of that love, then all is in harmony. If however we cannot do this and the past is brushed under the carpet or we move from one heartache to another without dealing with the issues at hand, then we are not free and we are unable to give all of ourselves to a new relationship for we are still entangled with the past. When we can acknowledge the value of a relationship, the lessons we learned and how we grew and if we can separate out our own fates from those we love and from within the family, then a space is created for love to grow. And it is okay if it becomes easy.

Within an intimate relationship there is a great simplicity in saying 'I will follow you' and submitting to the love that exists allowing the love and trust to flourish and grow. The reluctance and inability to do this and to acknowledge previous partners and fates leads to a fast food equivalent of relationships, with sex replacing intimacy and a subterfuge to the plot of the dynamic between the masculine & the feminine. It is very difficult and perhaps not so wise to ignore or flaunt the natural state of being within the dynamics of a relationship. It is worth remembering that when you enter into a relationship with somebody you are also aligning your family and ancestral lineage to theirs. So when you look at them if you are able to look and accept them and their family 'I can see this is part of who you are. I accept all of who you are.' There is a greater depth of connection and intimacy possible and it also negates the need for the partner to have to defend against aspects of their family. This is because with our intimate relationships we are creating our own version of our family of origin and merging it with that of our partner. For it to succeed we must be willing to accept our partner's family as being part of who he/she is. To be willing to see all aspects of them, exactly as they are is to truly give yourself in service of the relationship. If you can do this whilst simultaneously showing them your true self and accepting your own family as part of who you are, then nothing can stand in the way of your relationship and your love.

Chapter Six

Children

The patterns within a family flow from generation to generation as the children unconsciously follow the fates of those that have gone before. They can become entangled with the unseen, the unacknowledged and the excluded within the family lines, carrying the burdens and the pain of their parents and the previous generations. Children appear to do this out of a great love and loyalty to the family system and attempt to put right and balance the family field, often at the expense of themselves. This loyalty to the system can take many forms, whether it is through entanglement within their emotional behaviours and connection, through excluding themselves from the family in place of those who have perhaps been excluded or by an effect on their physical or emotional health where they attempt to 'save' a parent or family member from a particular fate/illness by carrying this in their stead. As such the focus of many constella- tions is to bring the family field to a point of balance that acknowledges and gives place to the entanglements, whilst at the same time keeping the children safe, thus ensuring that the patterns at play within the line can be seen and the future gener- ations can continue on freely and at peace in their place.

The arrival of new life to a family line irrevocably changes that line. The changes that occur to an individual as they become a parent are immeasurable. The individual is no longer able to view themselves as simply an individual and separate any longer. They become more aware of the ties that bind. They become aware on some level of their place within their own family as well as the connection to the family of the Mother or Father of their child. And so it is that the child that comes in senses 'what is there' within their parents, their siblings and the other family members within the family field. This blind loyalty and magical thinking of the child is also extended into the realms of the parental relationship. As discussed in the previous chapter there is influence on an adult's emotional relationship choices and experiences from their parents' relationship patterns as well as their own personal relationship patterns. This influence becomes rooted into the psyche of the individual from childhood. There is a natural flow for daughters to move from the sphere of influence of their Father to their Mother at a certain age and for the son to move from the Mother's influence to the Father. This movement can be interrupted when one or other of the parents is entangled within a previous relationship or when one parent tries to alienate the other parent and influence the child's emotional bond. This kind of behaviour can lead to eating disorders and depression within the child as they struggle with their internal loyalty to both parents. If they attempt 'cut' a parent out of their life for whatever reason they are in effect cutting out an aspect of themselves.

When working with children there are several different threads of entanglement that I have observed both in group and individual sessions time and again.

Where a child is tied to a previous partner of the Mother or Father and is representing them within the family system

Where a child is carrying the guilt and pain associated with an aborted or miscarried sibling or the early death of a sibling

Where the child is experiencing the effects of adoption either within the present or previous generations

Children & Parents

We have explored some of the ways in which previous loves of one or other of the parents can influence the later emotional life of an individual in the previous chapter, but I think it is worth noting here the immediate effect on a child of an unacknowledged previous partner or an acrimonious break up of a parental relationship. In such cases the child will often develop behavioural issues that may be disruptive to the family as a whole as well as to the child's education and learning.

I recently worked with a young woman called Suzanne who had a pattern of controlling and aggressive relationships. She had split up with her most recent partner; it had been a physically and emotionally abusive relationship. They had a 3 year old son who was not eating. Suzanne came for the session as she was worried that her son was becoming ill. When we set up the constellation, the representative for the son withdrew from both his Father and Mother, he described a feeling of restlessness and grief. He looked down at the floor away from both of his parents and was visibly drawn to the realm of the dead. Suzanne was looking at her son and refusing to look at the father, she felt both afraid and angry in his presence. The father's representative said that he felt pushed out and wanted to walk away. He felt great anger when he looked towards Suzanne. I asked Suzanne to look to her son's Father and say:

'In spite of everything you are his Father and I am his Mother. This we will always share'.

When the son heard this he was able to turn around and face the direction of his parents.

I then asked Suzanne to connect with her son and say:

'I love that I can see so much of your Dad in you. It is okay if you are like your Dad.'

When Suzanne could release her relationship to the husband but still acknowledge him as the Father, this drew the son closer and he looked and felt relieved. When she was able to connect with her son and acknowledge that his Father was part of who he was too, then he was able to draw closer to both his Mother and Father and connect with them, looking both of them in the eye. The next day her son started to eat. It has taken some further work and encouragement from Suzanne whilst he is eating, acknowledging both herself and the father within the child, but the effect has been extremely positive. When a child feels they have to exclude a parent, they equate that in some way to excluding an aspect of themselves and the easiest way for them to do that is often to refuse to take nourishment for themselves, or to eat to please one parent but then make themselves sick out of unconscious loyalty to another.

Another way in which a child will react to the exclusion of a parent (or the previous significant love of one of the parents) is to represent them within the family. In effect saying to the other parent 'I am better for you than them'. When this happens severe behavioural issues can be displayed by the child. Laura came for a session to explore the dynamics of her relationship with her fourth child Tom. Laura had six children in total, her eldest three children to her first husband and her youngest three children to another partner who she was no longer with. Tom was the first child from her second relationship. Tom, who was eight years old at the time, was a very angry boy and was being educated at home to avoid some of the behavioural problems that had occurred in the school environment. We set up the constellation including Laura, her six children and both fathers. Tom's representative was very agitated and drawn towards the first husband, he couldn't settle within the constellation and would shift his focus from the first husband, to his father and then his mother. The mother couldn't look at either her first husband or her second partner and shielded herself behind her children. The second partner was withdrawn from the constellation and felt sick, he said that he would like to disappear. When I asked Laura to look at her first husband (who had been abusive), Tom stepped in front of her to stop her. Tom in this situation had taken on the

logical impact on fertility and sometimes the root of unexplained infertility, particularly secondary infertility, is found within personal happenings as opposed to a systemic entanglement. For example non-symptom infertility can often be linked to the mother's draw to previous children that she has either aborted or miscarried. In the case of secondary infertility (where at least one child has been successfully carried to term but there are fertility issues with conceiving and carrying another child), a contract made with one's self after a difficult birth or a systemic entanglement to a previous family member can be at work.

More people are turning to In Vitro Fertilisation (IVF) as a solution to their fertility issues. IVF is a medical process where egg cells are fertilised by sperm outside the womb. The process involves hormonally controlling the ovulation process, removing eggs from the woman's ovaries and letting sperm fertilise them in a fluid medium. The fertilised egg is then transferred to the patient's uterus with the intent to establish a successful pregnancy. The first successful birth of an IVF baby, Louise Brown, occurred in 1978. In terms of the realms of science and research, this is relatively 'new' and various studies exploring many different possible effects of IVF are regularly being published. I was interested to read research papers investigating a possible link to Aspergers syndrome and autism in IVF babies.

An estimated 1% of all American babies are now born each year through in vitro fertilization (IVF) and that figure is 1.5% in the UK. But perhaps IVF and other fertility treatments are solving one problem while creating another. Particularly in the case of non-symptom infertility, if there is a systemic entanglement which is affecting fertility, by bypassing what is there and using other methods to conceive, you could hypothesis that the unseen fate will pass to the child or will play out within the family in some other way. In a recent study, Dr. Ditza Zachor of Tel Aviv University's Sackler School of Medicine reported a strong link between IVF and mild to moderate cases of autism. According to her research 10.5% of 461 children diagnosed with a disorder on the autism spectrum were conceived using IVF, a significantly higher number than the 3.5% autism rate in the general Israeli population. I find this particularly interesting because when I have previously worked with individuals or families wishing to explore the dynamics of autism for a family member, within the constellation setting the child or individual who is autistic is very often drawn to a missing sibling or siblings who have been aborted or miscarried. When there is a history of loss of children, whether that is due to abortion, miscarriage or death of a child, the effect on the Mother is difficult. Often it is as if part of the Mother goes with the child or children that have been lost. In the case of IVF, where there are often incidences of miscarriage etc prior to beginning the cycle of IVF, there are inevitably 'failed' cycles of treatment resulting in the experience of further miscarriage, not only putting the parents under greater emotional strain and stress but also systemically creating more grief, and in some cases unacknowledged grief, within the family field. This grief can be too great for the Mother to bear, she will often find it too painful to 'see' the children she has lost, feeling only the pain of the hole that is left. In cases such as this the children that follow and survive are often entangled within the family system with their missing siblings, effectively 'seeing' them for the Mother as she herself is unable to. This is in addition to whatever fate was perhaps affecting the parent's fertility in the first instance.

This can be further complicated in the case of IVF treatment where embryos that were created in a cycle of treatment but not implanted within the womb are frozen for future use. A decision must be made at a future point by the parents whether to destroy or donate these embryos to other families. This could potentially have a similar effect to abortion or adoption on the family field, which would tie in with the studies linking an increase in Autism to IVF babies.

Of further interest is research suggesting that women who have had difficulty conceiving or who have undergone IVF treatment successfully or otherwise are more prone to depression. In my opinion this is linked to the observation within constellation that a Mother who has lost children through abortion and miscarriage is drawn to those children in the realm of the dead and that she is less able to see her surviving children who are living.

"There is evidence that mild to moderate psychological symptoms associated with infertility may persist even after a woman conceives. These findings emphasize that infertility is a clinical condition with complex psychological issues, and suggest that conception through ART may be associated with an increased risk of depression symptoms during pregnancy and the postpartum period. Clinical decisions should take into account this increased risk; clinical care for women who are planning to conceive through ART should include psychological support, consultation, and, if necessary, intervention, even after they successfully conceive." Fertility and Sterility (Monti et al, 2008)

Depressive symptoms during late pregnancy and early parenthood following assisted reproductive technology (Monti et al, 2009) .

In exploring these theories I am not suggesting that techniques such as IVF are negative or should not be utilised, I am instead suggesting that an awareness of the systemic entanglements and the possible effects on the children may be beneficial to the family as a whole and that exploring what is there within the family may free up the children for the future generations.

Children and Adoption

Although there are many positives to the adoption process, not least the provision of a safe and nurturing home for a child, adoption itself can be a very difficult thing for all involved. In terms of familial experiences, the birth family loses a child, the child is separated and loses their parents and the adoptive parents must (in some cases) face their own grief associated with their fertility/loss of previous child and accept this new child as part of their family. These are fairly big issues for all to come to terms with and. though it is possible to navigate through these issues (and many people do), some do come up against stumbling blocks that create an entanglement within the family. When a couple adopt because they cannot have a child and their 'need' to have a child is so intense that they turn to adoption, the adopted child in some cases then 'fills' the hole that exists within the family, effectively carrying the burdens or fates that exist there. In such cases where there is a systemic reason for the infertility and the child takes this burden on board, the adoptive parents' relationship will often suffer and the parents may split up as their loyalty is tied. Ultimately the adoptive child is tied to their birth parents and they display great loyalty and love to the birth family, often unconsciously waiting for them to come back to get them. When adopting a child, the need of the child to be looked after must come first and respect for the place of the birth parents must be given. If that can be done then the child and the adoptive family can harmonise with one another. If the adoptive parents attempt to step in the place of the birth parents then the child's loyalty is torn and problems may lie ahead.

Major issues triggered by adoption are loss, rejection, guilt and grief and these affect the birth family, the adoptee and the adoptive family. A sense of identity crisis can trouble the adoptee as they try to figure out who they are. They may forge intense romantic relationships at an early age in order to feel part of a family or unit where they themselves belong. There is often an experience of not fitting in or not being equal to the other siblings within the family, the birth hierarchy of the family being more dominant than the added 'adoptee' child.

For the birthparents, it's the loss of their child. Whether they have chosen to give it up for adoption or if indeed it is a decision that was taken out of their hands, they will still grieve for the loss of the child. This will have an impact on any other children they may have and will also perhaps create an entanglement where individuals within the following generations will be tied to the fate of the adopted child and the grieving parent.

The adoptive parents can feel rejected by 'parenthood'. The grief over not having children can be overwhelming for the adoptive parents and grief is also obvious in the parents who lose their child to adoption. It is how this grief is dealt with and acknowledged that can determine the impact of the adoption on all concerned.

Effects of Adoption on the Adoptee

Some adoptees can suffer from attention deficit disorders, eating disorders and alcohol abuse. There can also be a tendency to seek alternative lifestyles as they attempt to find their true self. There is often a great longing for the birth parents, the birth mother in particular. Observing adoption within constellation, you will often see the individual is waiting for the birth mother to come back, a refusal on some level to move forward or to take their place, as they wait for the connection that their soul craves.

The experiences of the adoptive parents can be difficult as they now have a permanent reminder of the infertility they have experienced, perhaps a failed pregnancy or the death of their child. Some live in fear of the day they will have to tell their child that they are adopted or feel rejected if their adoptive child seeks their birth family. The grief of the adoptive parents can continue as the child grows up as the adoptee can never fully meet the expectations of the adoptive parents, particularly if they are attempting in some way to replace a child that they have lost.

With the birth parents giving up their child, whether it is through choice or a forced decision, a deep seated sense of loss can be created. Often the loss is never fully acknowledged by the birth parents or the birth parents' family members, thus it gradually becomes a 'family secret'. A great grief for the child and a deep and secret longing and wondering about the child's life can go on under the surface of everyday life. And so a family secret is born as the birth mother decides whether she can speak of her child within the next relationship, to her subsequent children and to those important people who share her life's journey with her.

Adoption in the Previous Generation

Amanda came to a group seminar because she had experienced a difficult relationship with her mother when she was alive. She felt that the relationship she shared with her daughter was heading in a similar direction and wished to improve the connection with her daughter. Amanda's mother had been adopted and had no connection with or knowledge of her birth family, despite many years spent searching for information. We set up a constellation initially with just Amanda and a representative for her Mother. The Mother was very agitated and found it difficult to see or focus on her daughter. Amanda became irritated with her Mother's behaviour, she behaved in a very childlike way and Amanda was behaving as if she were the Mother and not the daughter. I then placed the Mother's birth Mother within the constellation and the relief displayed within the Mother was palpable. However Amanda became angry and agitated towards the birth Grandmother. The Mother and the Mother's birth mother stood looking at one another for a long time. The Mother smiled. Then a seriousness came over her, I asked her to say to her birth mother:

"I have been waiting for you."

At this point the birth mother began to cry and withdraw from both Amanda and her daughter. I placed the birth Father within the constellation. The birth mother becomes more peaceful when the birth father is placed, he looks lovingly towards the birth mother and when he looks at his daughter he describes feeling a great longing in his chest. The birth mother says to her daughter (Amanda's mother) "I couldn't keep you". At this Amanda's mother takes a deep breath and says that yes, that feels right. We continued to work through the constellation and Amanda's mother was able to say to her birth mother: "I'm not going to wait anymore." At this point she was able to fully connect with Amanda, her daughter. Amanda became very emotional at this point. After some further work involving the adoptive family, we finished with Amanda stepping into her maternal ancestral line, with her daughter taking the line on in front of her and her mother, birth grandmother and birth great grandmother taking the line through to the ancestors. Amanda felt very strong in her place and was able to feel accept the support and love from her mother and pass that on in turn to her daughter.

The examples that we have explored in this chapter are from the current or close generations but events in the past can have considerable bearing too. Perhaps an interesting family to explore in terms of several generations of effects on children over the years would be The Kennedy family. Looking at the four generations of The Kennedys, with the first generation descending from the marriage of the Irish-Americans Joseph P. Kennedy, Sr. and Rose Elizabeth Fitzgerald, you uncover a family that is prominent in American politics and government and often referred to as the American royal family. The family has suffered a series of tragedies, particularly within the fourth generation, sometimes called "the Kennedy curse", including the assassination of brothers John (JFK) and Robert, and the controversial Chappaquiddick incident (referring to circumstances surrounding the death of Mary Jo Kopechne, whose body was discovered underwater inside an automobile belonging to Senator Edward M. Kennedy. The body and the car were found in a tidal channel on Chappaquiddick Island, Massachusetts, on the morning of July 19, 1969. After the discovery, Kennedy gave a statement to police saying that on the previous night Kopechne was his passenger when he took a wrong turn and accidentally drove his car off a bridge into the water. After pleading guilty to a charge of leaving the scene of an accident after causing injury, he received a suspended sentence). And there were also four airplane crashes (Joe, Jr., Kathleen, Ted and John, Jr.), three of them fatal. A great deal of tragedy for one family line that suggests there are fates unseen and entanglements not acknowledged within the line and often there are unseen victims at the very root of a supposed curse. The indignity suffered by a soul or group of souls becomes a powerful force that ripples through the generations when it is not acknowledged. The solution comes when you can humbly look to the root of the situation and see the victims, see the loss, acknowledge the pain and with honour give them a place in your heart.

Working with constellation is like working with the fabric of the soul. Weaving the threads of life through your fingers, tracing the patterns and entanglements, a gentle touch is required. You cannot simply cut out what you do not wish to see; instead you must find the right place for it and for yourself. Everyone has the right to belong within the family. Everyone has a place.

Chapter Seven

Victims & Perpetrators

The Costa Family

It is 1942 and Italy is under German occupation. In a little village in the South lives the Costa family, consisting of the mother, father and five children. The relationship between the mother and father is strained, they are both alcoholics and the father is violent towards the mother and the children. Money is tight and the father manages to earn a little on the black market, this he spends on drink. A lot of the household responsibilities fall to Anita, the eldest daughter at 10 years old. The youngest is 4 year old Paolo; he liked to play in the square with his friends. This afternoon their mother is with her friends drinking and their father is with the children in the square. Or rather he is sitting drunk at the side of the square. He is wearing a uniform and is pointing a rifle at the children as they play, pretending to shoot them and shouting obscenities. The reason he is drinking, he claims, is out of embarrassment because of his son Paolo's behaviour. Earlier this day he witnessed Paolo accepting some chocolate from a German officer. The father struck Paolo hard and then proceeded to get drunk taunting his son in front of his friends. Perhaps unknown to the father his little boy was becoming increasing withdrawn and saddened by the behaviour of both his parents. This is what Anita believes. Anita is watching her little brother Paolo today but has so many other responsibilities, other siblings to keep an eye on and chores to do. Her mother has disappeared for the day, leaving her in charge of feeding the family again. She turns to return to their home leaving Paolo in the square with his friends and their drunken father. In the very moment she turns to begin her journey home the father does something that she just cannot comprehend. He takes a grenade from his pocket and throws it at his son, shouting "Boom! Make papa proud you little shit!" The grenade hits Paolo in the face and then falls to the ground. Paolo begins to cry. Then Anita watches as Paolo picks up the grenade and says to his father in a quiet voice "For you Papa" as he pulls out the pin...

How does reading about the fate of Paolo make you feel? Can you see the child as he stands there? Can you feel that emotion and pain? Violent death within a family sends ripples of emotion out to the generations that follow. Three generations on the death of little Paolo is still impacting the family. The generations that follow have been affected by his abuse, his violent death, the fate of the father and mother as well the guilt that Anita suffered. She blamed herself. She was haunted by the image for the rest of her life. Even though she eventually married and had children of her own, part of her always felt that she should have stopped the father, she should have protected her brother, she should have been killed instead...anything except the harsh reality of the brown eyed little brother that she loved blowing himself up in front of her very eyes. Anita's great granddaughter came for a family constellation session to explore her destructive relationship patterns and experiences of 'not being seen'. She also suffered from depression throughout her life. She was tied to the fate of little Paolo and through bearing witness to his story and his life, by seeing him as he was and giving him his place she was able to move forward herself and take the first steps towards her own place... When someone in a family is 'unseen' when their story isn't told and their voice is unheard the generations that follow unconsciously follow the fate of the excluded individual. The events of previous generations can have far-reaching implications on the choices you make today. War and violence, the loss of children or parents – even if it happened generations ago – are all events that can leave a subconscious imprint on your actions. Sometimes there is a need to go back before you can move forward. Going back and finding out who these people were and what they did will often give you a clue to who you are and perhaps why something is happening in your life. Think about your own family now... The lives that have been lived... the fates of those that have gone before you. Think too about your own life and path... What do you see when you close your eyes?

Observing Constellations

Within the constellation setting the most common theme that appears is where an individual is tied to the fate of someone who has gone before them, who is not at peace within the realm of the dead. The prevalence of the dynamic of victim and perpetrator within the constellation setting is extraordinary. The entanglement that is created from an event where someone is responsible for taking the life of another yet will not 'look' to the victim is a very strong phenomenon and the ripples that flow down the family lines can affect many generations to come. The events that create such an entanglement do not have to be a great family secret, situations of war and violence and the deaths that occur due to them can be devastating for many generations of a family, not only in terms of the victim's family but also the perpetrators.

Audrey Hepburn's life choices and in particular her work with charities is very interesting when you take in to account her family background and experiences of World War II. She was born Audrey Kathleen Ruston in Brussels, Belgium. In 1935, Hepburn's parents divorced and her father, a Nazi sympathizer, left the family. Both parents were members of the British Union of Fascists in the mid-1930s, according to Unity Mitford, a friend of Ella van Heemstra and a follower of Adolf Hitler.

In 1939, her mother moved Audrey and her two half-brothers to their grandfather's home in Arnhem in the Netherlands, believing the Netherlands would be safe from German attack. In

1940, the Germans invaded the Netherlands. During the German occupation, Hepburn adopted the pseudonym Edda van Heemstra, modifying her mother's documents because an 'English sounding' name was considered dangerous, with her mother feeling that "Audrey" might indicate her British roots too strongly.

By 1944, Hepburn had become a proficient ballerina and she secretly danced for groups of people to collect money for the Dutch resistance. She later said, "The best audience I ever had made not a single sound at the end of my performances." After the Allied landing on D-Day, living conditions grew worse, and Arnhem was devastated by Allied artillery fire that was part of Operation Market Garden. During the Dutch famine that followed in the winter of 1944 people starved and froze to death in the streets. Hepburn's half-brother, Ian van Ufford, spent time in a German labour camp. Suffering from malnutrition, Hepburn developed acute anaemia, respiratory problems, and oedema. In 1991 Hepburn is reported to have said "I have memories. More than once I was at the station seeing trainloads of Jews being transported, seeing all these faces over the top of the wagon. I remember, very sharply, one little boy standing with his parents on the platform, very pale, very blond, wearing a coat that was much too big for him, and he stepped on to the train. I was a child observing a child."

Hepburn's wartime experiences later led her to become involved with UNICEF. Her war-time experiences inspired her passion for humanitarian work, and although she had worked for UNICEF since the 1950s, during her later life she dedicated much of her time and energy to the organization. From 1988 until 1992, she worked in some of the most profoundly disadvantaged communities of Africa, South America and Asia. In 1992, Hepburn was awarded the Presidential Medal of Freedom in recognition of her work as a UNICEF Goodwill Ambassador.

Speaking of her long-standing work with children's charities,

Hepburn said, "I speak for those children who cannot speak for themselves, children who have absolutely nothing but their courage and their smiles, their wits and their dreams."

Upon setting up the constellation it becomes clear that she is pulled to the realms of the dead and the unseen victims within the family connected to the war and that there is a great guilt at her own survival. Through bearing witness to the victims in the realm of the dead via her service to the charities that she is dedicated to she is able to access a sense of peace but the drain upon her from doing it this way is very great. When you look outside of the family and the family fates to clear the entanglement that exists within the family, you will be greeted with an endless line of souls whom you can help 'save', her drive and passion to give voice and to bring attention to the unseen is rooted in the unseen fates of the souls of the victims within the family field.

This is something that is very common in families where there has been the perpetration of others. The generations that follow are often drawn to the fates of the victims and display behaviours or patterns that indicate that they are "sacrificing" themselves in some way, giving up their place so that the victim or victims may be seen again and carrying the grief and the guilt that has previously been unexpressed within the family. Within the constellation setting you will often see someone who is 'unseen' by those around them, someone who feels that they don't have a place. They are tied to the unseen and displaced victims. You will also observe those that are tied to the perpetrators, who will often experience great anger and draw this towards themselves and become entangled with destructive and violent relationships. Those who are tied to the perpetrator or who have that fate within their family often as an attempt to address the karmic balance will become involved in the field of healing whether this is through the medical profession, social care or alternative and complementary therapies. Such individuals can experience chronic burn out as they attempt to 'heal' others as a way of bringing peace to their family lines. Unfortunately they are at no point addressing their own family entanglement; they instead are faced with an endless queue of individuals who require energy and support and they find themselves becoming weaker and weaker. This too is a form of self sacrifice to appease the familial entanglements.

Omaha Beach, June 6th 1944

"I feel despair. I cannot see the way forward. Everything is dark and I am helpless. There is no hope." Sophia comes for a constellation and this is how she feels on a daily basis. She is very judgemental of herself as she feels she has no real reason to be having these emotions, on the surface everything is fine, she has a partner and they have a daughter together. Yet in her heart she feels she just doesn't belong. In fact she wishes she weren't here. "It would be easier for everyone if I just disappear". Acknowledging that this is how she feels and speaking the words aloud brings a certain clarity to her and she can see and feel the ties of love that bind her to her husband and child. Yet the ties to the fates of those in the realms of the dead are stronger.

When we set up the constellation it became clear that she was heavily drawn to her Father and his fate. She could not see her husband or child. The child's representative was very emotional and felt like she too did not have a place. The representative felt her legs grow weaker and weaker and she sank to the ground, saying the she too wished to disappear. The Father was attempting to shield her from the mother.

Sophia's father had served during World War II. He was an officer with the British Navy and he was responsible for sending nine waves of American soldiers, young men, on to Omaha Beach on landing craft before he himself disembarked on to the beach. Very few men survived. The beach is now known as "Bloody Omaha" because of the 2,200 casualties suffered by the

American troops who landed there on D-Day in 1944. This was something that Sophia's father never really recovered from. Sophia recalls revisiting the beach with her Father when she was a child but he could not set foot on the shoreline. For him he could still see the blood and the bodies of the men who had died that day. She remembers being shocked at seeing the emotional response of her Father, this coupled with her natural tie to the family fates led her to make an internal promise that she would sacrifice herself in order to give a place to the war dead, to appease her father's guilt. In essence she was trying blindly to make it all better in the only way a child knows how.

We added representatives for the victims who had lost their lives. Sophia immediately sank to her knees alongside them, whereas her Father's representative simply could not look. He became very cold and began to tremble as did Sophia's daughter. The little girl was following in the footsteps of her Mother and attempting to relieve the burden of her Mother and Grandfather by carrying it herself. I asked her to say: "Please Granddad, you are bigger and stronger that me. Please help me with this." The child also said to her Mother: "Please stay with me Mum. I can see them too". After a while the Grandfather slowly turned around and he looked towards the victims. His body shook quite violently and he began to weep. Eventually he was able to look at them. I brought in representatives for his ancestors prior to the war and did the same for the victims to enable both of them to be in places of strength. They embraced and the victims and Sophia's Father felt a great sense of peace and relief. Sophia and her daughter looked upon them for a long time and then said: "Thank you. I will remember you in my heart." They were both then able to return to Sophia's husband, the child's father and look to the future together.

Remembering the dead is so important. When they are not seen and they are not at peace they have an effect on the living as if they were still alive. When the circumstances of their death are such that they have sacrificed their life so that others may live, if they have sacrificed their life for their beliefs or their country or indeed if someone has taken life in such circumstances, it adds an extra dimension to the entanglement and the pattern that inevitably flows down the family lines. We see life as precious but if another's life is not valued and we are tied to that fate then we are unable to value our own life or to accept the sacrifice of others. We are unable to submit to their fate. Peace comes when the victim and perpetrator can be seen and acknowledged within their respective family fields again, when the fate is placed with them, in turn the family members are able to look to both the victim and the perpetrator and accept that this is part of who they are and the system becomes whole again.

Murder and Exclusion

The 1950s in Glasgow was a dangerous time. Gang culture was rife and as well as territorial tensions rooted in gangs originating from different areas there was also a lot of religious tension within the city. The cities areas were segregated into Catholic and Protestant dwellings and there was little love lost between the two different cultures. In the North of the city, purely by chance, a young Catholic man called John met and fell in love with a young Protestant girl called Rosemary. The young man was from a well known family who controlled a very violent gang, his 3 brothers were more involved than he was but it was his mother who ruled the roost. No one dared defy her and she ran the 'business end' of the various protection rackets, gambling dens and fight clubs that was their livelihood. She also had the final say on the murders committed.

John and Rosemary conducted their relationship in secret, there was much at stake. After several months Rosemary discovered that she was pregnant. That sealed things in John's mind. He prepared himself and his love to elope and marry, leaving the city and his family behind. He confided his plan to the one brother he trusted. Unfortunately his trust was betrayed. His brother went straight to their Mother and shared the news of the relationship and pregnancy that defied that family. The Mother acted swiftly and ordered an attack on Rosemary, an attack intended to result in her losing the child. However in the violence that ensued Rosemary lost her own life as well as the life of her unborn baby. John survives but is devastated, a broken man...

Fifty years on and Gayle, the daughter of the brother who betrayed John comes for a constellation session. She has suffered from depression on and off her whole life. She has experienced a string of destructive relationships. She has one child and she kept the pregnancy a secret from the child's father, she had a fear of losing her baby and so opted to live alone just her and her son. She moves around a lot, not comfortable to stay in any one place for too long. She experiences being 'unseen' by others but finds it safer that way. Her father is in a mental institution, she is the only family member that visits him there. Gayle is tied to the fate of Rosemary and her unborn child and the dynamic within the family is such that Gayle is sacrificing her place and atoning for what happened to Rosemary whilst also representing the victim for her father as he holds the energy of the perpetrator. The crime was never brought to light, the victims were never given their place. Instead it was swept under the carpet. A family secret. An entanglement created that perpetuates throughout the perpe-trators and victims' family. Within such situations you will often observe an individual within the family who suffers greatly from mental health issues, who carries unexpressed guilt and grief. Reuniting the victim and perpetrator within the constellation and allowing them to see one another. Allowing the responsibility to be taken without judgement or blame is to move towards peace in the soul.

Murder and violent crime create such a heavy fate. When the victims are not seen the generations that follow can be drawn to them, they make efforts to bring them to light by sacrificing aspects of themselves whether that be success in their material life, denying themselves love or through their physical health. Some family members that are drawn to such a heavy fate are at risk of suicide and suicide itself can become a pattern in families that have experienced violent trauma in one form or another. When the perpetrator does not take or accept responsibility, when they cannot 'see' or face their victims or the victims family then they become very 'big' energetically. They overshadow other members of their family, making them feel small. The generations that follow that are tied to the fate of a perpetrator can carry a great anger that will flare up within them. They can energetically tower over their family members shifting the dynamic (for example treating their Mother as a child and behaving as if they are in fact the parent). They will often be involved in destructive, violent or manipulative relationships either as the victim out of contempt for themselves or as the perpetrator. And so the fates are carried forward...until the unseen are seen and the stories that haven't been told are heard. Bear witness to them.

Chapter Eight

Your Own Journey

You & Your Ancestors

Family constellation and ancestral patterns work is fascinating. As you have been reading through this book you have probably been thinking of your own family and your place within it. You will maybe have experienced reactions to some of the examples, a sense of familiarity or solidarity with some of the fates and entanglements described. Perhaps you will have pondered how to begin to work with your own family and ancestors...

If you think about your own life and the path that you are walking right now, how do you feel? As you have been reading the previous chapters, have you identified an area of your life that feels entangled? Do you feel grounded and in place when you think of your family? Do you feel happy and loved within your relationship? Can you look to the generations that will flow on from you with love and kindness?

If you have identified an area or an issue that you would like to gently explore and feel your way through then I have created a path for you to follow through your own family tree. If at any point it feels uncomfortable or overwhelming give yourself permission to stop and take a step back. The steps are intended to guide you through some of the entanglements and fates that my exist within your own family field, if you would prefer to do this in a more supported way then there are websites that will have lists of practitioners available in your area.

In Preparation

Before you start any of the following explorations set aside some time to notice and observe how you feel within yourself, how comfortable you are within your own skin at the beginning of the work.

Sit quietly for a moment and close your eyes. Let your breath come and go naturally and just sit in the moment...

How do you feel?

How does your body feel?

If you mentally scan down your body from the top of your end to the tip of your toes how does it feel?

Are there any areas of tension?

Are there any parts of you that feel physically uncomfortable as you do this?

Now pay attention to how you feel emotionally in this moment. Do you feel at peace? Are you feeling any emotions positive of otherwise?

Is it comfortable to connect with yourself in this way?

Are you in fact connecting with yourself? Do you feel grounded and present within your own body or do you feel disconnected?

It is important and often enlightening to take note of how you feel throughout this process when you tune in to your being in your natural 'relaxed' state. As you progress through the following work, I will suggest that you scan through your body, your thoughts and your emotions at various points so that you can become more aware of what happens to you physically, mentally and emotionally as you connect, engage and interact with different aspects of yourself and your family within the family field. If you are familiar with your own energy and state of being, then you will become more adept at noticing any shifts or changes that occur when you work within your own family field and will develop awareness of any fates and entanglements that you are connected to. If you find it difficult to scan through your physical body or your emotions then instead it can be extremely helpful to focus simply on your breath in your natural and compare this to what happens to your breathing when you interact and connect with different aspects of the family field.

Mother

Take a moment now. Close your eyes and think of your Mother. In your mind's eye see her standing before you. Feel your connection to her.

Breathe in that moment.

How does it feel for you?

What happens to your breathing here compared to how it feels in your natural state?

What comes in to your mind as you look upon your Mother?

Notice how your body and breath react to your conscious connection to your mother. Is it a comfortable and loving connection? Does any part of you feel tense or uncomfortable?

Can you sense the connection clearly or is it hazy, blurred or fragmented?

What happens if you say "You are my mother and I am your son/daughter"?

How does it feel? What happens to your breathing?

If you find this challenging then work through the relaxation steps from the beginning of the chapter again, ensuring that your energy is grounded within your body. Then go through the process of connecting again with your mother but this time around bring in your mother's parents (your grandparents) behind her. Take a deep breath and see how the connection is for you now.

Add in your great-grandparents, and then your great-great-grandparents and so on. As you work back through the generations notice how you feel emotionally and pay attention to your breathing and any tension or relaxation within your body. Focus on how it feels to connect with your Mother as you add in the previous generations behind or around you. At what point does it become a comfortable and positive experience for you to connect and acknowledge your place within the maternal line?

As you look at her or feel your connection to her can you imagine your mother as a child herself, growing up within her family with all the entanglements therein?

Can you imagine her hopes, her fears and her dreams? Do any of them resonate with your hopes, fears and dreams?

See her in your mind's eye meeting your Father, beginning their relationship together.

Now look upon their combined hopes and dreams for the future, do they have to compromise or sacrifice for one another?

For their families?

Now see her in your mind's eye as she discovers she is pregnant with you, how does that feel?

Can you see the different directions in which she is pulled?

Her different loyalties and entanglements?

See or feel the sacrifice that is made as she is transformed from woman to mother, what price does she pay to be your Mother?

What price do you pay to be her child?

Go back to the beginning now...

Close your eyes again and think of your Mother.

In your mind's eye see her standing before you again.

Feel your connection to her once more.

Breathe in that moment...

How does it feel for you now?

Father

Take another deep breath.

Close your eyes and think now of your Father. In your mind's eye see him standing before you and take the time to really look and see him.

Feel your connection to him, feel it in your heart.

How does your connection to your Father feel for you?

What happens to your breathing here compared to how it feels in your natural state?

What comes in to your mind as you look upon your father?

Notice how your body and breath react to your conscious connection to your father. Is it a comfortable and loving connection? Does any part of you feel tense or uncomfortable?

Can you sense the connection clearly or is it hazy, blurred or fragmented?

What happens if you say "You are my father and I am your son/daughter"?

How does it feel? What happens to your breathing?

If you find this challenging then work through the relaxation steps from the beginning of the chapter again, ensuring that your energy is grounded within your body. Then go through the process of connecting again with your father but this time around bring in your father's parents (your grandparents) behind him. Take a deep breath and see how the connection is for you now.

Add in your great-grandparents, and then your great-great-grandparents and so on. As you work back through the generations notice how you feel emotionally and pay attention to your breathing and any tension or relaxation within your body. Focus on how it feels to connect with your father as you add in the previous generations behind or around you. At what point does it become a comfortable and positive experience for you to connect and acknowledge your place within the paternal line?

Have a think about what it might feel like to change from boy to man to Father.

What sacrifices may be involved?

What does the boy have to leave behind to become a man?

What price does one have to pay to become a Father?

Go back to the beginning now...

Close your eyes again and think of your father.

In your mind's eye see him standing before you again.

Feel your connection to him once more.

Breathe in that moment... say within yourself "my father"

How does it feel for you now?

If you don't know your mother or father or perhaps don't feel connected to them, then the following exercise may help. Spend some time sitting in front of a mirror or looking at a photograph of your face. Study all your features, the colour and shape of your eyes, the curve of your mouth. Half of you is made up of your mother and your mother's line and half of you is made up of your father and your father's line. Even if you don't personally know them or know exactly what they look like there are parts of you that do. There are parts of you that know them very well. By firstly looking for the familiar features that you have that connect in and mirror the family members you know of or resonate with, you can then look at those features that you do not instantly recognise. The features that perhaps come from family members you are yet to connect with and acknowledge. By seeing what is there in a new way you can start to accept the parts of you that previously have remained hidden from yourself.

Siblings

Your place within your family is interwoven around your connection with and to your siblings. Your place within the 'order' of your siblings has influence various aspects of your life. It can be incredibly difficult to hold a place within the family that is not your place for example holding the place of the first born when you are in fact the second and your elder sibling was miscarried or aborted. Imagine standing in the place of the eldest child, with all the expectation that goes along with it, when you are in fact the second or third child. 'Missing siblings' can have an impact on the surviving siblings in terms of their emotional communication with their living siblings, their parents and their ability to communicate effectively and succeed in the world outside of the family. By the term 'missing sibling' I mean a child that is missing from the family through a miscarriage, an abortion, a still birth or an untimely death. The loss of a child can be so painful that it is unbearable for the parents to 'look' at the now missing child, however the energy of the child, the soul of the child still exists and if the parents cannot look often the other siblings will look in their stead and so an entanglement is created. The missing children belong to the family, even if the loss was in the very early stages of pregnancy and the mother herself was unaware, and the energetic imprint of the child or children will still be there and their absence felt by the others. In such cases where the missing siblings are early losses, and given that approximately one third of pregnancies begin with a twin pregnancy and end with a single foetus (known as vanishing twin syndrome) this is quite a high possibility, the effects of the missing siblings are enhanced or diluted depending on the other fates and entanglements that exist within the family field.

Prepare for this exploration by taking some time to sit in your natural state and relax your mind, your body and your breath. Ensure that you are sitting in a chair where you are supported or laying down flat on the floor. This exercise will require you to take note in particular of how you feel physically within your body and the subtle changes that may occur as we work through your sibling line, so it is worth spending some time before you begin acclimatising yourself to how your physical body feels in its natural state. For example:

Do you feel balanced on both sides of your body?

Do you feel a lighter or heavier on one side compared to the other?

Can you feel your feet or do you feel 'grounded' and within your body?

Do you feel comfortable in this your natural state?

For individuals who have siblings

In your mind's eye arrange yourself within your sibling line of living siblings, starting with the eldest on your right hand side through to the youngest on your left hand side (or ending with yourself if you are in fact the youngest). Work with your breath as you do this remembering to take nice deep breaths as you work your way through the line and feel your connection to each sibling in turn. So for example if you are the third of four children you will have your two older siblings next to you on your right hand side and the youngest next to you on your left. As you sense your place amongst them work through the above questions again:

Do you feel balanced on both sides of your body?

Do you feel a lighter or heavier on one side compared to the other?

Can you feel your feet or do you feel 'grounded' and within your body?

Do you feel comfortable in this your natural state?

If you know of any missing siblings through your family history or previous therapeutic work then add them in to the sibling line at this stage.

If you do feel lighter or heavier on one side or unbalanced then it is often a sign of missing and unacknowledged siblings within the line. I have noticed that it is often the case that if there is a particularly difficult relationship with a sibling or siblings that there is a hidden dynamic of a missing sibling at play. Connect with your sibling line through your mind's eye or through sensing and feeling your way along it by noticing your physical and emotional response. Begin to add in a missing sibling in to the line in the places that feel blank, numb or uncomfortable for you. As you do so say to them

"I can see you now."

"We both belong here."

"You have a place within my heart."

Then check in again with how you feel physically and emotionally. Keep working your way down the sibling line adding in any missing siblings until you feel that it has come to a point of balance. When you feel you have reached that point of balance and you feel at peace within it is time to acknowledge and honour each of your siblings in turn and also to affirm your own place in the line. You can either do this is your mind's eye or through lighting candles to honour each sibling (you will need a small candle or tea-light for each sibling).

Start with the first child saying:

"You are the first and I am the (your place)" and light the candle for them.

Then

"You are the second and I am the (your place)" lighting a candle for them too and so on down the line. When you are lighting the candle for yourself say aloud "I am the (your place) and I take my place".

You can repeat this acknowledgement exercise whenever you feel the need to.

For only children or individuals who have been adopted

When you are unsure if there are any missing siblings or, in the case for those who have been adopted, if there is uncertainty over whether or not any other siblings exist then the focus when working your way through the potential sibling line is very much on how you feel and react throughout the process. As you work through the initial steps to calibrate your internal reactions and then notice how you feel on each side of your body, adding in a sibling where you feel there is a gap or a space and gently pay attention to how you respond emotionally and physically until you feel grounded, at peace and fully balanced within your place.

Re-connecting

Once you have found and accepted your place within your sibling line it is interesting to notice how you feel re-connecting with your mother and father and the feminine and masculine lines. Connecting with the parents and the ancestral lines is often easier and more comfortable when an individual is secure and grounded within their own place in the sibling line.

It is helpful to note at this point that when you are working through the above steps for the connection to the parents as well as the sibling that when the link or connection to a family member or family line itself is difficult or just not there or when it appears blurry or partially obscured then the indication is that they are entangled with another fate and that is why they cannot be seen or felt clearly.

As you work through your link to your mother, father and the ancestral lines again take time to notice your breath, what happens when you connect to each person? Do you hold your breath, can you feel tension within your body? What happens if you exhale deeply? How far away from the family member(s) do you have to be in order to connect to your sense of self and feel balanced?

If you are still finding it difficult to make the connection in a way that feels comfortable then a useful exercise to try is to bring in several generations of your ancestors as you make the connection with your parents. Working back through five generations of your family and bringing them into your awareness would be as if you had stepped in to a room of over a hundred people. You can imagine or feel them encircling you or perhaps see the lines stretching out in front of you. Experiment with how many generations of your ancestors you need to bring in to your awareness and energetic field in order for you to feel more comfortable with the roots of who you are and you lineage. As you feel the connection to your ancestors say to them simply "yes".

If when you are working through your connection to your family lines you have a sense that someone or something is still missing or if the connection remains blurred then we can look further to see who is missing from the picture. In chapter seven we explored the impact of the unseen on the family field. In your mind's eye you can at this point invite in those who are 'unseen' within the family (whether it is individuals from within the family that have been excluded or indeed individuals from outside of the family whose fates have become entangled through perpetration of them by a family member). As the unseen are seen and given their place it is important again to affirm your own place. You both belong.

Love & Relationships

At the end of a relationship or at the beginning of a new one it can be a natural reaction to want to brush the past aside and start afresh, pushing away our hurt, grief, negative emotion and experiences as we dive into the new. However, if a previous relationship and partner aren't acknowledged and if we don't give place to the love that existed then it is very likely that the experiences of the first relationship will flow into the second and so on. When you fall in love with someone, when you form an intimate relationship with them, you form a tie that cannot be broken and that tie is even stronger when children are involved. Your fates and family patterns become intertwined and less of you becomes available for any subsequent relationships. The likelihood that you will become involved with a new partner that holds similar family fates and entanglements to those of your previous partner is also increased. So how do you begin to heal and clear this, bringing peace and creating space for love? You look to your first relationship, your first love and really look to see what is still there for you.

Take a moment now and cast your mind back to your first love, your first serious relationship…

Remember how you felt when you first met and fell in love…

The promises you made to one another…

The plans for the future you made together…

Now remember how you felt when it ended…

How did you feel when you found out that they had moved on…had children…

How do you feel about that now…

Perhaps they haven't moved on…how does it feel to think of them as stuck…

How would it be to wish them well…

How would it be to wish their children well…

How do you think your ex-partners look upon you? Upon your family? What would you ask of them if you could?

Even if our perception of a relationship is that it is of no real consequence, it doesn't necessarily mean that the other person involved will feel the same. If you are experiencing a repetition of behaviour and experience within your intimate relationships or if you feel that you are not seeing your current partner clearly, or them you, then you can work with your relationship patterns to clear previous fates from your current love.

Spend some time thinking about the relationships that you have had in your life, starting with your first love. If you need to, write down a list and include everyone you have been involved with, whether it felt important for you at the time or not. Then guide yourself through the steps to get to your natural relaxed state, working with your breath and allowing the tension and stress to leave your body. Then see your first love in front of you and feel the connection to them. Notice what happens to your breathing and if your body becomes tense or remains relaxed as you connect with them. See them as they were when you first met and allow yourself to feel the way you did when you first fell in love with them. Say to them

"You were important for me."

"Thank you."

"You were the first."

"What was between us has gone now."

"The promise is broken."

"I'm ready to let you go now...please let me go too."

Then work your way through any other relationships until your current relationship. Take time to feel how you respond as you connect to each in turn and explore any entanglements that may exist between you. When it feels as if the connection is sticking or the entanglement isn't moving forward, then it can be helpful to bring in the connection to your parents and family line as if they are standing behind you and to see your (previous) partner with their family behind them. There are often similarities in fates within the families of those we become intimate with and this can further deepen the entanglement.

Relationship dynamics can be further complicated if the relationship was abusive or if there are children involved. When you have children with someone, even though your intimate relationship may end, you will always be connected through your children and it is important for all concerned, particularly the children, that this is honoured. Being able to say "In spite of everything you will always be the father/mother of our children and I will always be their mother/father" is enormously freeing for the children.

Your Children Born and Unborn

The patterns and entanglements flow down the line in many cases from parent to child, so looking and feeling your way through the connection you have to your children, both born and unborn, can be extremely enlightening as to the fates that are currently at play within your family field. Children who carry a burden or fate for either a parent or ancestor are doing so out of a great love and an unconscious loyalty to the family as a whole, it is not a reflection on how much you love your children or how good a parent you are.

Before you begin to explore the connection to your children and the continuation of the family line, remember to allow yourself some space to relax your body and mind. Focus on your breath and take some nice deep breaths, breathing in positivity and breathing out any tension or stress within your body.

Next, either within your mind's eye or through emotionally and physically feeling the experience, connect to your children. See or have an awareness of them standing in front of you (if you have more than one child, see them in a row on front of you by order of age from eldest on the left to youngest on the right). As you connect with each of them in turn take a deep breath and see how it feels to simply smile at them from your heart.

What happens in your body when you do that?

What happens to your breathing?

How is it with each child?

Now say to each of them in turn:

"You are my son/daughter and I am your mother/father."

"I accept you as my child and you can have me as your mother/father."

How does it feel when you say that?

If you have had any miscarriages that you know of, add the child or children to the line saying "I accept you as my child and you can have me as your mother/father". You can do the same with any aborted or adopted children, this may be very emotional and you may need support throughout the process.

It's okay if it gets easier now...

I love the moment at the end of a constellation where the field comes into balance, the ancestors are at peace, the family members are acknowledged and the individual in question stands in their place free from the burdens and fates of those that have gone before them. They stand there instead with the support and strength of their family line, aware only of their own potential and energy. They physically relax into themselves and the sense of being at peace is tangible. This is the moment to remember. This is the point to move forward from. This is when we say to ourselves "It is okay if it gets easier now..." For many this is also when the hard work starts. The sense of change can be disconcerting for many. How strange it can feel to be unencumbered by another's fate, to stand in your own place, supported and with the knowledge that you are smiled upon by your ancestors as you make your own way. Removed from the supportive environment of the therapy room or workshop space, it can feel very daunting indeed and fear can kick in. If you feel that, if you are aware of what is really there within the family and your connection with it, then the biggest step to take is to allow the family and the ancestors to be at peace. To take a deep breath, to acknowledge that you are bearing witness and accepting what is and what has been and that you are now ready to truly take your place. It really is okay if it gets easier now. As you assure yourself of this, feel your connection to your family and ancestors, bring in the generations before you and feel or see them standing around you in a circle, physically bow your head down to them and simply say "I take my place".

References

Bert Hellinger, Colleen Beaumont. To the Heart of the Matter: Brief Therapies Dec 2003

Bert Hellinger and Colleen Beaumont. Farewell: Family Constellations with Descendents of Victims and Perpetrators. Jan 2003

Seligman, M. E. P. In J. Buie (1988) 'Me' decades generate depression: individualism erodes commitment to others. APA Monitor, 19, 18.)

Leon, D A; McCambridge, J: Liver cirrhosis mortality rates in Britain from 1950 to 2002: an analysis of routine data.

Ursula Franke and Colleen Beaumont. In My Mind's Eye: Family Constellations in Therapy and Counselling. Jan 2003.

Roy, Nielson, Rylander et al., 2000. Family history of suicidal behavior and earlier onset of suicidal behaviour.

William R. Lovallo et al. May 2006. Reduced Amygdala Activation in Young Adults at High Risk of Alcoholism: Studies from the Oklahoma Family Health Patterns Project

Bert Hellinger, Jutta Ten Herkel. Insights: Lectures and Stories. 1 Jan 2002

Seligman, M. E. P. In J. Buie 1988. 'Me' decades generate depression: individualism erodes commitment to others. APA Monitor, 19, 18.

Judith Rich Harris. The Nurture Assumption. Oct 1999.

About the Author

Nikki Mackay is a family constellator, sound therapist, Reiki master and an experienced pyschic medium.

As a medical physicist she has researched the effects of energy healing on the nervous system and published her findings within the scientific and new age community. An experienced intuitive and teacher she established a Holistic retreat centre in Scotland and developed the centre for 3 years. She is now the editor of 'The WitchHiker's Guide' magazine, a guide to all things alternative in Scotland. She also teaches seminars and works with individuals exploring family and ancestral patterns.

Her aim is to bridge the gap between Science and the new age and she keeps that in mind in everything she does.

She currently lives in Glasgow with her partner and their son.

www.flybroomstick.co.uk

BOOKS

O is a symbol of the world, of oneness and unity. In different cultures it also means the "eye," symbolizing knowledge and insight. We aim to publish books that are accessible, constructive and that challenge accepted opinion, both that of academia and the "moral majority."

Our books are available in all good English language bookstores worldwide. If you don't see the book on the shelves ask the bookstore to order it for you, quoting the ISBN number and title. Alternatively you can order online (all major online retail sites carry our titles) or contact the distributor in the relevant country, listed on the copyright page.

See our website **www.o-books.net** for a full list of over 500 titles, growing by 100 a year.

And tune in to myspiritradio.com for our book review radio show, hosted by June-Elleni Laine, where you can listen to the authors discussing their books.

MySpiritRadio